Property of Jesus

'I bear on my body the brand-marks of Jesus.'
Galatians 6:17, NASB

Selwyn Hughes
Revised and updated by Mick Brooks
FURTHER STUDY: IAN SEWTER

© CWR 2014. Dated text previously published as *Every Day with Jesus: The Owner's Stamp* (September/October 2001) by CWR. This edition revised and updated for 2014 by Mick Brooks.

CWR, Waverley Abbey House, Waverley Lane, Farnham, Surrey GU9 8EP, UK
Tel: 01252 784700 Email: mail@cwr.org.uk
Registered Charity No. 294387. Registered Limited Company No. 1990308.

Cover image: CWR
Quiet Time image: fotosearch
Printed in England by Linney Print

MIX
Paper from
responsible sources
FSC® C015900

Every Day with Jesus is available in **large print** from CWR. It is also available on **audio and DAISY** in the UK and Eire for the sole use of those with a visual impairment worse than N12, or who are registered blind. For details please contact **Torch Trust for the Blind**, Tel: 01858 438260. Torch Trust for the Blind, Torch House, Torch Way, Northampton Road, Market Harborough LE16 9HL.

A word of introduction ...

This issue of *Every Day with Jesus* was originally conceived in the late sixties when a member of Selwyn's congregation gave him an Amplified Bible. He opened it up to one of his favourite verses, Galatians 6:17, which reads: 'From now on let no person trouble me [by making it necessary for me to vindicate my apostolic authority and the divine truth of my Gospel], for I bear on my body the [brand] marks of the Lord Jesus [the wounds, scars, and other outward evidence of persecutions–these testify to His ownership of me]!' Even at that time he was struck with the thought of the brand marks of Jesus, testifying of His ownership.

Never has there been such fierce competition for brand recognition, brand identification and brand placement than there is today. The overwhelming message of advertising is to lure you into a brand lifestyle. Corporate companies want you to become the walking embodiment of their products.

The idea of branding and identification is not a new one, and here Selwyn shows how, in following Jesus, we become identified with Him, we belong to Him, not in a slavish under-the-thumb condemnatory relationship, but as heirs; sons and daughters of the living God. In this relationship God imparts to us His own branding and characteristics so that, remarkably, we become more like Jesus! None of us are perfect but we are all on the Way. In this issue Selwyn explores some of the ways in which God imparts to us His brand and characteristics so that not only are we recognised as having 'bought into' His lifestyle, we are also identified with Him.

Mick Brooks, Consulting Editor

Free small group resources to accompany this issue can be found at www.cwr.org.uk/extra. The *EDWJ* Facebook community is growing! To join the conversation visit www.facebook.com/edwjpage **f**

The brand marks

FOR READING & MEDITATION – GALATIANS 6:1-18
'I bear on my body the marks of Jesus.' (v17)

The theme for this issue of *Every Day with Jesus* is based on the intriguing statement made by Paul recorded in our text for today. He claimed that he bore branded on his body 'the marks of Jesus', or, in the words of the Moffatt translation, 'the owner's stamp of the Lord Jesus'. Paul, as you no doubt know, suffered physical torture and beatings because of his loyalty to Jesus, but he understood the marks which these beatings left on him to be not just scars but a vivid reminder that he was now branded – owned by Jesus.

Of course, the brand marks of Jesus were infused not only onto his flesh but into his emotional and spiritual life also. Today, the likelihood of being scarred with the marks of physical suffering because of our testimony for Jesus depends to a large extent on which country we live in. But all of us, whether or not we expect to endure suffering, could ask ourselves: How deeply are the marks of Jesus branded into our spiritual, emotional and mental attitudes and personality?

Even though we may not be called, as was Paul, to carry the outward signs on our flesh, we are most certainly called to carry it in our inner beings – to have it 'branded'. Perhaps you have had the marks of Jesus temporarily painted on and not permanently fixed in – therefore they have not remained. The attractions and 'brands' the world has to offer may be drawing you. You need something that will brand you forever before God and your fellow human beings so that no longer will there be any mistaking of your identity. Would you like to bear the inner brand marks of Jesus that reveal you are His property?

FURTHER STUDY

Exod. 21:1-6;
Acts 4:1-13

1. How did the servant show outwardly that he was the property of his master?

2. What was noteworthy about Peter and John?

Gracious and loving Father, may this wandering, wavering Christian life of mine be transformed. I want to be branded so that I may be unmistakably the property of Jesus. Make these next two months not only a time of challenge but also a time of change. Amen.

Forgiveness - the first mark

FOR READING & MEDITATION - LUKE 23:32-43

'Jesus said, "Father, forgive them, for they do not know
what they are doing."' (v34)

Yesterday we spoke of the need to have the characteristics of Jesus not temporarily painted on but branded in so that no longer will there be any mistaking of our identity before God and our fellow human beings. Perhaps this thought has challenged you so much that something within you is causing you to hesitate. You shrink from any idea of a 'brand' as being recognised and identified with Jesus. However, you will hesitate no longer when you consider what being branded is. We can be branded with the marks of Jesus. Could anything be more wonderful than that?

FURTHER STUDY

Gen. 50:15-21;
Acts 7:54-60

1. How did Joseph show Christlike forgiveness?

2. How did Stephen bear the marks of Jesus - inwardly and outwardly?

When we say we must have the marks of Jesus branded into us it is the same as saying that we should have Christlikeness sown into the texture of our beings – and that can never be done to excess.

What are the 'brand marks' of Jesus? It is those inner qualities and characteristics that reveal the heart of Christ dwelling within us. We shall look at a number of them as we proceed, but we begin by focusing on this: the willingness to forgive all injuries and offences. In one of his books, Sir John Seeley said that the most outstanding characteristic of a Christian is the willingness to forgive injuries. The prayer that Jesus uttered, recorded in our text for today, is probably the most amazing prayer ever spoken, for it embodies the most humble and yet strong spirit ever shown: 'Father, forgive them, for they do not know what they are doing.' Today God wants to give you that same spirit – the spirit of forgiveness which pardons injuries. I beg you, let Him do it. Retaliation and harbouring of resentment belong to a dead past.

O Father, impact me deeply. I relinquish now all my hurt and resentment, and all desire for retaliation. From now on, let no anger or unforgiveness trouble me. I bear Your brand. Amen.

We are seeing that one of the marks of Jesus is the forgiveness of injuries and offences. We are to be characterised with that same spirit, allowing it to be instilled so deeply within us that we instinctively refrain from retaliating or harbouring resentment. Some, of course, don't consider this realistic, seeing it as far removed from the realms of possibility. A letter once sent to me included these comments: 'Whenever I am hurt by someone, I find it extremely difficult to forgo all thought of revenge. I cannot argue with the fact that a forgiving spirit is a healthy one, but such a condition is to be found only in saints, not in Christ's ordinary disciples.'

Though I sympathise with the issue, I do not know of any verse in the New Testament which differentiates between saints and ordinary disciples. Granted a consecrated heart, Jesus can infuse His spirit of forgiveness deep into anyone's nature. Listen again to Jesus' advice: 'Love your enemies, do good to those who hate you, bless those who curse you, pray for those who ill-treat you.' Hard as it may sound, it is amazingly possible.

During World War II, a group of Belgian teenagers were reciting the Lord's Prayer together in a church. After the words, 'Forgive us our trespasses,' they paused before continuing with the rest of the sentence. They were wondering how they could forgive those who had ruined their country. As they paused, a voice behind them said: 'As we forgive those who trespass against us.' When they turned they saw that the speaker was the king of Belgium, who had lost everything – except his soul.

FURTHER STUDY

2 Kings 6:15-23;
Luke 22:47-51

1. Contrast Elisha and the king of Israel.

2. How did Jesus do good to those who hated Him?

Lord Jesus, You who forgave even those who hammered You to a cross, help me to be characterised by that same spirit of forgiveness. For Your own dear name's sake. Amen.

Resentment – wrong responses

FOR READING & MEDITATION – EPHESIANS 4:29–5:2

'Get rid of all bitterness, rage and anger … Be kind and compassionate to one another, forgiving each other' (vv31-32)

Now we have established that one of the characteristics of Christ is the forgiveness of injuries and offences, how do we put this principle into practice, which is what today's passage suggests we do? Over the years I have catalogued some of the unhealthy routes Christians take in attempting to deal with anger and resentment. Permit me to share them with you again.

One way is to suppress negative feelings into forgetfulness and try to act as though we no longer have them. This route only drives the feelings into the subconscious mind where they work as subconscious resentments. To suppress resentments, however, does not resolve them but allows them to work their perniciousness at a much deeper and more dangerous level in the personality. All resentment must be brought to the surface and honestly faced.

FURTHER STUDY

Psa. 5:1-12;
Heb. 12:14-15

1. How did David deal with his feelings?

2. Why should we avoid bitterness?

Another unhealthy way in which people handle resentment is to express their negative feelings by giving the perceived offender a 'piece of their mind'. No doubt one can get temporary relief by 'blowing one's top', as we say, but it is not the better option. Expression is not the remedy – it is dealing merely with the 'symptom' instead of the 'disease'.

Yet another way is to run away from the circumstances which caused the resentment. A doctor treating a patient for nervousness and insomnia discovered that the man greatly resented his mother-in-law. The doctor recommended a month's stay in a clinic where he would be away from the mother-in-law. Good advice, but not quite good enough. Much improved, the patient returned home, but within days all his previous symptoms started up again.

O God my Father, help me to see that where resentment is concerned I am probably dealing with something so deep-seated that it is unhelpful to attempt to heal it lightly. Help me to go to the roots and find release there. For Jesus' sake. Amen.

FOR READING & MEDITATION - 1 PETER 3:8-17

'Do not repay evil with evil or insult with insult, but with blessing'
(v9)

Yesterday we considered three routes which are, in the long term, unhelpful when dealing with resentment.

Yet another, which a number of people follow in order to deal with their resentment, is to work out their negative feelings through some form of activity. One woman remarked: 'When filled with resentment, I go to the piano and bang out my resentment through Mozart's sonatas – with apologies to Mozart.' Once I asked a particular group how they handled resentment. In response a man admitted: 'The way I deal with my resentment is to punch a pillow until all the anger has subsided.' Another said: 'I go for a brisk walk or dig the garden.' I do not deny that some relief is gained from these practices; they give temporary relief and act like a steam valve in a pressure cooker. However, they do not tackle the root causes.

Another route that people use in handling resentment is to nurse it in their minds. A woman once told me: 'I know it is unhealthy to push my resentments down into my subconscious, and I know also that it is wrong to express them, so the way I handle them is to hold them in my mind where they can do no one any harm – I simply chew on my resentments.' A good motive – but bad practice. Resentments that are nursed or chewed upon will spill over into all of one's mental and emotional attitudes. They will seep through into the whole of life and corrode one's own soul – as well as the souls of others. All of these methods I have catalogued are, in effect, attempts to heal over a boil. And to heal over a boil is a dangerous act – it may drive the poison further in. Poison must be drawn up and out.

FURTHER STUDY

2 Sam. 13:10-14; 22-29; 15:10-14; Jer. 6:13-15

1. Why did Absalom become guilty of murder and treason?

2. How may we be deceived?

O Father, the more I ponder this problem of resentment, the more I see how deeply its roots can entwine themselves within me. I cannot deal with it alone; I need Your help. Please brand me now with Your spirit of forgiveness. Amen.

A ladder out of resentment

FOR READING & MEDITATION - ROMANS 12:9-21

'Do not be overcome by evil, but overcome evil with good.' (v21)

Perhaps you have been thinking over the past two days: 'If the routes discussed are not the way to overcome anger and resentment then just what is the way?' Here are a few simple ideas for starting the climb out of the pit of resentment.

First, accept that all resentment is unhealthy, even if apparently justified. If you try, you can make out a good case to yourself to justify resentment. But, justified or unjustified, resentment is unhealthy and often leads away from living as you were originally designed to.

FURTHER STUDY

Matt. 18:21-22; Luke 22:31-34

1. How did Peter try to limit forgiveness?

2. How did Jesus deal with Peter's imminent betrayal?

Second, surrender all your resentment to God and consent for Him to take it away. Don't fight your resentment, but surrender it to the Lord. A single woman who was dominated by her mother used to rave against her in great outbursts of anger and resentment. She and her mother lived in separate apartments and couldn't even eat meals together. One day the daughter surrendered her resentment to God and became a transformed woman. Notice, I said in the statement above, 'consent for Him to take it away'. Some people expect God to come down into their hearts and uproot resentment without any effort on their part. God will do His part, but you too need to be willing to do your part.

This does not mean being liberated from resentment is the result of willpower alone. It is God's will for you to be free of your resentment – now make it your will also.

Third, after surrendering your resentment to God, actively forgive everyone you resent. If it helps, write down their names on a piece of paper, and say: 'Lord Jesus, as You have forgiven me, so I forgive _____ now in Your precious name.'

O God my Father, I would be rid of all that corrodes my soul. I consent now to be delivered from the last tiny root of resentment. I know You will it – now I will it too. Thank You, my Father. Amen.

CWR Ministry Events

PLEASE PRAY FOR THE TEAM

DATE	EVENT	PLACE	PRESENTER(S)
6 Sep	Handling the Pressure - Insight into Stress	Waverley Abbey House	Beverley Shepherd
19-21 Sep	Women's Autumn Weekend - Finding Freedom	Pilgrim Hall	Liz Babbs
20 Sep	Ideas for Small Group Leaders	WAH	Andy Peck
23-25 Sep	Bible Discovery Midweek: The Ωmega Course	WAH	Philip Greenslade
25 Sep	Hearing God's Voice	WAH	Andy Peck
26 Sep	Discovering Your Spiritual Gifts	WAH	Andy Peck
27 Sep	Insight into Self-Harm	WAH	Chris Ledger
1-3 Oct	Coaching and Mentoring	WAH	Beverley Shepherd and Andy Peck
6-10 Oct	Autumn Retreat	PH	Sandra Warner
9 Oct	Life and Times of Jesus	WAH	Andy Peck
10 Oct	Deeper Insights into MBTI ®	WAH	Lynn and Andrew Penson
11 Oct	Personality, Prayer and Spirituality	WAH	Lynn and Andrew Penson
13-17 Oct	Woman to Woman	WAH	Ministry to Women Team
16 Oct	The Bible in a Day	WAH	Andy Peck
17 Oct	What Next for New Christians? Growing Commited Disciples	WAH	Andy Peck
18 Oct	Insight Day: Godly Assertiveness	WAH	Chris Ledger
18 Oct	Living Singly for God's Glory	WAH	Julia Morgan and others
22 Oct	Women's Autumn Day: Untangled	WAH	Jen Baker
Oct-Dec	Developing Pastoral Care	WAH	Andy Peck
23 Oct	Signs on Revival (Prayer Evening)	WAH	Andy Peck

Please also pray for students and tutors on our ongoing **BA in Counselling** programme at Waverley and Pilgrim Hall and our **Certificate and Diploma of Christian Counselling** and **MA in Integrative Psychotherapy** held at London School of Theology.

For further details and a full list of CWR's courses, phone +44 (0)1252 784719 or visit the CWR website at **www.cwr.org.uk** Pilgrim Hall: **www.pilgrimhall.com**

Forgiveness is power

FOR READING & MEDITATION - MATTHEW 5:38-48

'If all you do is love the lovable, do you expect a bonus?
Anybody can do that.' (v46, *The Message*)

Yesterday we examined some initial steps we can take in order to deal with resentment. If, after meditating on these steps, you still have difficulty in this matter, then consider this story which I heard some time ago – one that spoke deeply to my own heart.

An Armenian nurse was out walking one evening with her brother when they were attacked by a gang of Turks, who killed her brother before her eyes. The gang escaped and were never apprehended. Some months later, while on night duty at the hospital where she worked, she recognised one of the patients as the man who had murdered her brother. Her first feeling was of revenge. The man was extremely ill – hovering between life and death. She realised that with the slightest neglect he would die. His life was absolutely in her hands. But instead of revenge, she decided for Jesus' sake to forgive him. She fought for his life and won, nursing him back to health.

FURTHER STUDY

1 Sam. 24:1-11,16-19

1. Contrast the attitudes of David and his men.

2. What effect did David's actions have on Saul?

When he recovered, she told him who she was. The man looked at her in astonishment and asked: 'Why didn't you let me die when you had me at your mercy?' 'I just couldn't,' she replied. 'I am a Christian and my own Master forgave His enemies who crucified Him. I must do the same for His sake.' 'Well,' responded the Turk, 'if this is what it means to be a Christian, I want to be one also.'

Could you do what that nurse did? It isn't easy, but it can be done – with God's help. Let Him brand deep into your soul this mark of Jesus – the forgiveness of injuries. Retaliation and harbouring of resentment are things that belong to the past. From now on you can bear His brand.

Gracious Master, may this brand of Yours - the forgiveness of injuries - be infused within me and remain there forever. From now on I will let no anger or resentment take root in me. Gladly I bear Your brand. Amen.

A servant's heart

FOR READING & MEDITATION - MARK 10:35-45

'For even the Son of Man did not come to be served, but to serve'
(v45)

Now we move on to examine another mark of Jesus with which we can be branded: the mark of authentic servanthood. In the passage before us today, Jesus is explaining that His primary reason for coming among us was not to be served, but to serve. The first-century world in which Jesus found Himself was filled with position-seekers – Caesars, Herods and others – whose goal in life was to exploit their position for personal advantage. Not so Jesus. His crowning mark was that He cared more about what happened to others than about what happened to Himself. Listen to His words on another occasion, as He declares yet again the main reason for His coming to the world: 'I am among you as one who serves' (Luke 22:27).

Over the years I have written many times of the one major objective to which God is committed in the lives of all His people: 'For God knew his people in advance, and he chose them to become like his Son' (Rom. 8:29, NLT). No sooner do we find ourselves in the family of God, following conversion, than the Father sets about the task of branding in us the qualities which characterised His Son.

James Irwin, the astronaut, tells how he felt after returning to earth following his successful moonwalk. 'I knew,' he said, 'that people would consider me a celebrity, but I am not really a celebrity, I am simply a servant. I am here now on Planet Earth to share what I have experienced, that others might know the glory of God.' At that momentous time in his life God revealed to Jim Irwin a basic principle that many of us would do well to learn: we are not celebrities – we are servants.

FURTHER STUDY

Deut. 10:12-13;
Acts 27:31-28:3

1. What does God ask of us?

2. How did a hero become a servant?

O God my Father, brand me with the same serving and giving qualities that characterised Your Son. Help me to make this my life goal: to become, not a celebrity, but a servant. For Your own dear name's sake. Amen.

Everyone is a servant!

FOR READING & MEDITATION - MATTHEW 20:20-28

'whoever wants to become great among you must be your servant'
(v26)

We continue meditating on the need to be branded with the marks of Jesus, and the characteristic we are focusing on at the moment is the mark of authentic servanthood.

As long as I live, I shall not forget the fear that gripped my heart when, many years ago, I came face to face with this important truth. From the time I first became a Christian I had assumed that the words 'servant' and 'leader' were antonyms, not synonyms. I remember saying to myself as I read for the first time the passage which is before us today: 'Me? A servant? But I want to be a leader. Lord, what does this mean?' I imagine it must have been a great shock to the disciples also to be told that in order to be the greatest they must be the servant of all. They didn't want to serve – they wanted to be served.

FURTHER STUDY

Acts 9:36-40;
Acts 13:36

1. How did Dorcas serve others?

2. What did King David do?

Jesus takes advantage of the request made by the mother of James and John to teach His disciples the difference between His teaching and the philosophy of the age in which they are living. Society, both then and now, functions on the principle that there are distinct lines of authority. As Jesus put it: 'their great men exercise authority' (v25, RSV). The implication behind these words, I think, is that great men not only exercise authority, but delight to do so. They enjoy the feeling of power that authority brings them. But then He adds: 'It shall not be so among you.' What does He mean by that? Simply this – that in God's kingdom the situation is reversed: we may be called upon to exercise authority, but our delight lies not in lording it over others; it lies in ministering to others. And the difference is crucial.

O Father, give me, I pray, a servant's heart. Help me to get hold of the truth that the way to the top in Your kingdom is not through striving, but through servanthood. In Jesus' name I pray. Amen.

The 'celebrity syndrome'

FOR READING & MEDITATION - 1 CORINTHIANS 7:17-24

'he who was a free man when he was called is Christ's slave.' (v22)

The American pastor and writer Charles Swindoll says that the subject of servanthood is one of the forgotten issues in Christianity today. Is he right? I believe he is. Regrettably, there doesn't seem at times to be much of a servant mentality in some sectors of the Church. We are so caught up in the 'celebrity syndrome' that we lose sight of the fact that our primary calling in Jesus is to be servants.

Perhaps you are saying to yourself at this moment – as indeed I did when I first came across this truth: 'But there must be leadership in the Church in order to get things done.' Quite so. But it's leadership that arises out of a servant's heart. It really doesn't matter to me at this moment what kind of church government you believe in, but I am concerned that everyone who is involved in the ministry of leadership sees himself or herself as one who serves. Without this attitude the Church is no different to the world.

Many years ago, when I was pastor of a church in London, a young man came to me and said: 'I believe God has called me to a leadership role in His Church. Will you permit me to exercise my gifts and calling right here in this community?' This was my response: 'If God has called you to a leadership role – fine. But first show us how good you are at serving. Give out the hymn books at the door for a year, and if you do that well then perhaps we can discuss your call to leadership at the end of that period.' I never saw him again. Some time later I heard that this young man had given up going to church and seemed to have drifted into spiritual oblivion. He fixed his eyes on the wrong goal.

FURTHER STUDY

Matt. 23:11-12;
Eph. 6:5-9

1. Who will God appoint as leaders?

2. How should we view all work?

O Father, teach me to be more interested in serving than in being served. Help me to make it my goal, not to get others to serve me, but to seek out ways in which I can serve them. Amen.

'Who's the greatest?'

FOR READING & MEDITATION - LUKE 9:37-50

'An argument started among the disciples as to which of them would
be the greatest.' (v46)

We turn our thoughts again to Jesus' definition of
greatness, which we first saw in Mark chapter 10:
'whoever wants to become great among you must be your
servant, and whoever wants to be first must be slave of
all' (Mark 10:43-44). The need to get a divine perspective
on this important subject of greatness is highlighted in the
passage before us today. Here Jesus' disciples were not only
clashing with each other, they were also clashing with the
outlook of their Master.

Of course, they all believed that what they were
fighting for was 'principle'. The self soon learns
that it cannot get its own way in the presence
of spiritual principles unless its assertions are
clothed with 'spiritual' arguments. Peter might
have claimed: 'I am one of the oldest in the group,
and besides, I was the one who made the great
confession of Jesus' Messiahship. The interests of
the kingdom demand that age and insight take
precedence.' Andrew might have argued: 'But
I knew Jesus before you did – and first come,
first in authority.' Then John might have said: 'I
am known to many of the elite in Israel, and if
we are to influence the nobility and bring them
into the kingdom of our Master then I must be
the one to lead.' Perhaps Judas also became involved and
reasoned: 'I am the one whom Jesus has put in charge of
the money, therefore I ought to be first.'

Whatever the actual words, we know that the kingdom
was in their speech but self was in their intentions. Each
tried to demonstrate his greatness, but all they succeeded
in doing was revealing their smallness. Always remember
– only the humble truly lead.

FURTHER STUDY

Num. 12:1-8;
1 Tim. 3:1-13

1. How could
Moses be
a humble
servant and
great leader?

2. What are
the qualities of
church leaders?

**O God my Father, how different Your Church would be if each
one of us could see that greatness consists not in getting, but in
giving. Brand that truth into my innermost being this very day.
In Jesus' name I ask it. Amen.**

'Toiling in rowing'

FOR READING & MEDITATION - MARK 9:33-41

'they kept quiet because on the way they had argued about who was the greatest.' (v34)

Over the past few days we have been seeing that greatness consists not in 'lording' it over others, but in desiring the best for others.

However, it is also true that everyone, deep down, longs to be great. Two small boys, both children of missionaries, were arguing over the respective greatness of their fathers. One capped it all by saying: 'My father teaches subjects at school that are so hard that even he doesn't understand them.' That settled the matter – his father was the greater and, by implication, he was also.

A certain man objected to the fine imposed upon him by the authorities for his drunken behaviour. Did he object because the fine was too big? No, he objected because it was too small. 'I shall never be able to lift my head among my colleagues,' he said, 'if all I receive is a small fine.'

This desire for greatness was built into us at creation. The great God, who fashioned us in His own image, could not have done anything less. Truly, greatness is our destiny. The trouble is, however, that we try to achieve greatness in ways that are contrary to God's design. We confuse greatness with recognition and worldly success and, as a result, grow small trying to be great. Nine-tenths of the difficulties in the Christian Church are the result of clashes between Christians, and nine-tenths of those clashes arise because they do not understand the true path to greatness. They do not want to serve; they want to be served. But it doesn't work. Like the disciples on the Sea of Galilee, we 'toil in rowing' (see Mark 6:48, KJV), trying to get to the land of greatness and ending nowhere.

FURTHER STUDY

Matt. 8:5-13; Luke 17:7-10

1. How did the great centurion serve his own servant?

2. What should be the nature of our self talk?

Blessed Lord Jesus, You who came not to be ministered to but to minister, help me to follow this model in my own life and ministry. For Your own dear name's sake. Amen.

Great truths - acted

FOR READING & MEDITATION – JOHN 13:1–17

'he poured water into a basin and began to wash his disciples' feet'
(v5)

We have already said that the disciples were probably nonplussed when Jesus presented them with the truth that in order to be the greatest of all, they must be the servant of all. Today we ask ourselves: How did Jesus get His disciples to acknowledge this seemingly unacceptable truth? Well, to put it simply, He modelled it himself.

Dr Alexander McLaren, that great preacher who lived in the nineteenth and early twentieth century, made this comment in one of his sermons: 'The greatest truths are not just spoken – but acted.' He went on to illustrate this point by saying: 'When Mary broke the alabaster box of precious ointment, she said nothing – but in her act she spoke volumes. When Christ hung upon the cross, His words were few, but His act had eternal repercussions. And when Christians take bread and wine in their hands and celebrate Christ's death, little is said but a lot is acted.'

FURTHER STUDY

Acts 18:1-4;
20:32-35;
2 Thess. 3:6-13

1. How did Paul act out the message of servanthood?

2. What model did he provide?

Now apply this principle to the incident we are looking at today, and what do we find? Difficult though it may have been for the disciples to accept the truth of Jesus' words, it was impossible for them to ignore the impact of His actions. The One who knelt before them was the Creator of the universe – God of very God. The disciples, in trying to be great, got nowhere. How powerfully this action of Jesus must have brought home to their hearts the lesson that the path to spiritual greatness lies along the route of authentic servanthood. When we forget greatness and bend with Christ to serve the rest – what happens? As we bend, we rise; the servant of all becomes the greatest of all.

Gracious Father, I kneel yet again at the feet of the Man who washed my feet. Brand into me that same spirit of humility so that I shall rise to know true spiritual greatness. In Jesus' name I ask it. Amen.

Small worlds turned upside down ...

a serious concern for many Christian families

When children first enter and then navigate their way through primary school, they must adjust to encountering new people and new demands. Some will also encounter bullying and a sense of isolation.

Primary schools are fast-changing places; they must serve the children from families of other faiths – and an increasing majority who come from families of no faith at all, which can make church-going children appear to others – and themselves – as somehow different.

CWR has launched a special publication called *Topz Tips for School* to focus on troubling issues faced by children in primary school.

To make this vital resource accessible to the greatest number of children – it has to be affordable. Experience tells us that a cover price of 99p is affordable, but publishing costs would necessitate a retail price of £2.99.

We need to subsidise each copy by £2. Every pound you can spare will be used to bridge the gap and set so many small worlds right again. I do hope that you can help. Our children truly do deserve all the help we can give.

Lynette Brooks

Lynette Brooks, Director of Publishing

Please fill in the 'Gift to CWR' section on the order form at the back of this publication, completing the Gift Aid declaration if appropriate.

True greatness

FOR READING & MEDITATION - PHILIPPIANS 2:1-11
'Your attitude should be the same as that of Christ Jesus' (v5)

We spend one final day meditating on the need to have branded within us the mark of authentic servanthood. Permit me at this stage to ask you a personal question: which of these two desires is the stronger in you – the desire to serve, or the desire to be served? If it is the latter then I suggest you spend as much time as you can meditating on today's reading, at the same time asking Jesus to transform your thinking and brand you with the characteristic of authentic servanthood. It is important to understand that servanthood starts with the right mental attitude. In the words of one preacher: 'Living differently begins with thinking differently.' The apostle Paul expressed this thought when he wrote: 'Do not conform any longer to the pattern of this world, but be transformed by the renewing of your mind' (Rom. 12:2).

FURTHER STUDY

John 8:28-29;
Gal. 5:13-26

1. How did Jesus combine greatness and humility?

2. How can we keep in step with the Spirit?

God's Word flowing through our thoughts can bring about the right mental attitude to servanthood. You see, our view of greatness is the acquisition of power; God's view of greatness is voluntary submission. Our idea of greatness is to be free from all restrictions; God's view of greatness is to become humble servants. Our view of greatness is immediate fulfilment; God's view is to see us being transformed into the likeness of His Son.

More often than not, right thinking precedes right acting. So bring your thinking in line with God's thinking – this very day. Again I say, servanthood starts in the mind. Make a positive decision to bring your views into line with God's views, and then let the Lord brand you with this mark of Jesus – the mark of authentic servanthood.

Lord Jesus, forgive me that I size up other people in terms of what they can do for me. Change me, Lord. Brand me with Your mark - the mark of true servanthood. For Your own dear name's sake. Amen.

Is life a constant struggle?

FOR READING & MEDITATION - PSALM 18:16-40

'It is God who arms me with strength and makes my way perfect.'
(v32)

As we continue considering the marks of Jesus we come to another characteristic of Christ which God wants to brand into us – inner strength and peace. There are some Christians, I know, who will part company with me here, because they believe that in this world we can never expect to find inner strength and peace. 'The Christian life is a struggle,' they claim, 'and we ought not to pretend that it is anything else.' The song they delight to sing is this:

Awake my soul, stretch every nerve …
Fight the good fight with all thy might.

FURTHER STUDY

Matt. 11:28-29;
Isa. 40:21-31

1. What is Jesus' promise to us?

2. What will happen to those who hope in the Lord?

This has some truth in it, of course. A famous psychiatrist once said: 'The perfectly adjusted person is the perfectly useless person. We must struggle against the *is* on behalf of the *ought-to-be*.' We dare not adjust ourselves too much to circumstances and things as they are, for that kind of adjustment would result in inner decay and death. Rather, we must grow and develop, and development involves a struggle against our environment, both inner and outer.

Yes, we are called to 'fight the good fight of the faith' (1 Tim. 6:12), but remember, it is a fight inspired by the faith which we are instructed to pursue (1 Tim. 6:11), and this will give us an inner calmness and strength amid the outer struggle. It is also a good fight: a fight that makes you tense and strained is not a good fight – it leaves you drained and exhausted. But the Christian fight involves us in a struggle that does not sap our energy; indeed, the very struggle produces greater inner strength and peace. How? The strength of the struggle pervades you and makes you even stronger.

Father, I am thankful that I need not be a strained, struggling soul with no centre of undisturbed calm within. Brand me with this quality too. For Jesus' sake I ask it. Amen.

How did Jesus live?

FOR READING & MEDITATION - LUKE 4:1-14
'Jesus returned to Galilee in the power of the Spirit' (v14)

Yesterday we said that the idea of the Christian life being one of inner strength and peace is one that some Christians find difficult to accept. Unfortunately, the view that the Christian life is a ceaseless struggle, with no inner peace and calm, has been responsible for leaving a trail of strained would-be saints whose lifestyle is singularly unattractive. The question we ask ourselves is this: Did Jesus manifest an inner strength and peace in the midst of adverse circumstances?

To this we can give an unqualified 'Yes'. We have but to turn to the New Testament to see that it was so. We see His life was one unending struggle – and also one of unending inner calm, confidence and strength. Take the moment when, at the age of 12, He was gently chastised by His mother for not keeping up with them when they left the city of Jerusalem. His reply – 'Didn't you know I had to be in my Father's house?' (Luke 2:49) – indicates an inner confidence that He was in the right place doing the right thing at the right time.

FURTHER STUDY

Matt. 27:11-14;
John 19:1-11

1. Why was Pilate amazed?

2. What did Jesus acknowledge?

But what about inner strength? That test came at the beginning of His ministry when He went into the wilderness to be tempted by the devil. After 40 days of fasting and temptation we might have expected Him to emerge in utter exhaustion. On the contrary, the account says that He 'returned to Galilee in the power of the Spirit'. Here was inner strength and calm – to the nth degree. That which was intended to weaken Him served only to strengthen Him. Isn't this the spirit you have been looking for – the spirit that meets everything that comes with inner strength and peace?

Yes, Father, this is indeed what I have been looking for - a spirit that meets everything and masters everything, and does so with strength and peace. Brand it deep into my being. In Jesus' name I pray. Amen.

'His way - not theirs'

FOR READING & MEDITATION - LUKE 4:14-30

'But he walked right through the crowd and went on his way.' (v30)

Yesterday we saw how Jesus manifested inner strength and calm when confronted by His mother in the Temple at Jerusalem, and also in the midst of the wilderness temptation. In today's passage we see that same spirit in evidence when, after returning from the wilderness, He announces in the synagogue at Nazareth the news that He has come to preach good news to the poor, freedom for prisoners and recovery of sight for the blind.

At first the people who heard Him were deeply impressed with His preaching: 'All who were there spoke well of him and were amazed by the gracious words that came from his lips' (v22, NLT). But Jesus would not permit them to continue with a mistaken view of His ministry, and quickly let them know how far He intended to go. 'God cares especially about such people as widows, lepers and even Gentiles,' He told them. With these words He cut right across their spiritual pride and prejudices, for every day a pious male Jew thanked God that he 'was not born a woman, a leper or a Gentile'.

No wonder the atmosphere changed from acceptance and admiration to anger and hostility. The people from the synagogue led Christ to the brow of the hill on which their town was built, with the idea of hurling Him over the top to His death. How did He react under the ensuing chaos? Did He fall apart and become an anxious wreck? Listen to what the account says: 'Then passing through the midst of them, He went His way' (v30, NKJV). Notice: His way, not theirs. His inner strength and peace was such that it must have shown on His face, causing the crowd to fall back and let Him pass.

FURTHER STUDY

Dan. 3:13-28;
John 6:14-15

1. Describe the attitude of the three Jews.

2. How did Jesus respond to admiration?

O God, I see the strength and peace that was at work in the life of Your Son. Brand these two qualities into me to such a degree that those around me may observe them clearly. Amen.

Both God and Man

FOR READING & MEDITATION - HEBREWS 4:1-16

'He's been through weakness and testing, experienced it all
- all but the sin.' (v15, *The Message*)

Over the past few days we have been observing something of the inner strength and peace which Jesus demonstrated during the time He was here on earth, and quietly we have been breathing a prayer that the same spirit might be branded into us.

Some critics of Jesus, however, have claimed that there are at least five places in the Gospels where He lost His strength and calm, and these instances, so they say, indicate that He was not quite the person we Christians suppose Him to be. The instances they give are: (1) at Lazarus's tomb, where Jesus was 'deeply moved in spirit and troubled' (John 11:33); (2) at the coming of the Greeks: 'Now my heart is troubled' (John 12:27); (3) in the synagogue: 'He looked round at them in anger' (Mark 3:5); (4) in the Garden of Gethsemane: 'He began to be sorrowful and troubled' (Matt. 26:37); (5) on the cross: 'Jesus cried out in a loud voice ... "My God, my God, why have you forsaken me?"' (Matt. 27:46).

FURTHER STUDY

Heb. 2:9-18; 5:1-9

1. Why did Jesus share our humanity?

2. What does this mean when we face difficulty?

Do these five instances mean there was a breakdown in Jesus' spiritual strength and confidence? Most definitely not. These instances, in fact, make the very thing we are saying more complete – for us. Suppose Jesus had been unmoved in these situations – what then? We would come away with the idea that Jesus faced all circumstances without difficulty or the desire to avoid them? In fact, He experienced the full range of human emotions but remained confident in His Father's trust and love. Had He sailed through every crisis with complete serenity, something would have been lacking; He would have shown us He was God, but we would never have seen that He was Man.

Blessed Lord Jesus, I am so grateful that when I come to You I am coming to One who has worn my flesh, measured its frailty and fully experienced how I feel. I am deeply, deeply thankful. Amen.

'Five-foot drops'

FOR READING & MEDITATION - 2 CORINTHIANS 4:1-18
'we've been thrown down, but we haven't broken.'
(v9, *The Message*)

We continue thinking about the importance of being branded with this third mark of Jesus – inner strength and peace. Today we ask ourselves: If we are branded with this characteristic of Jesus does it mean that never again will we experience negative emotions when confronted by the problems and disasters of life? The answer is 'No'. Jesus, as we saw yesterday, experienced a number of negative emotions in His life – pain, grief, anger and so on. He was not exempted from them – and neither are we.

What benefit is there, then, from being branded with His spirit of inner strength and calm? Dr Lawrence Crabb, a Christian psychologist, illustrated the point like this: imagine yourself standing on the edge of a cliff a thousand feet high and suddenly being pushed off. If you survived the fall you would doubtless be badly hurt – even shattered. Now imagine standing on the edge of a cliff which is only five feet high and, once again, someone suddenly pushes you off. How do you think you would feel then? Shattered? Hardly – it's only a five-foot drop. You are more likely to describe your feelings in terms of being shaken rather than shattered.

There's a big difference between a thousand-foot drop and a five-foot drop. Crabb says: 'A Christian who draws daily from the spirit of Jesus and lives in a close relationship with Him will never experience a thousand-foot drop, only a five-foot drop. He may be shaken, but he will never be shattered.' Can you see what he means? God has not promised that He will allow us to go through life unshaken, but He has promised to carry us through unshattered.

FURTHER STUDY

Job 13:14-15;
2 Cor. 1:3-11

1. How did Job view death?

2. How did Paul move from fear to faith?

O Father, every hour of this day deepen my consciousness of the truth that when I am branded with the spirit of Jesus there are no thousand-foot drops – just five-foot drops. In His name I ask this. Amen.

Quick adjustment

FOR READING & MEDITATION - 1 PETER 5:5-11

'the God of all grace ... after you have suffered a little while,
will himself restore you' (v10)

Today we return to the matter we looked at two days ago – the five occasions when, according to the critics, Jesus was bereft of inner strength and calm. On every one of these occasions we find Him shaken, but not shattered. What is more, on each occasion Jesus makes a quick adjustment to the situation and, although for a while He appears troubled and disturbed, within a short time He once again demonstrates His characteristic confidence in His Father.

Charles Richet, a great scientist and thinker, said:

FURTHER STUDY

Mark 14:32-42;
2 Cor. 12:7-10

1. How did Jesus adjust to difficulty?

2. How did Paul adjust to difficulty?

'It may sound contradictory, but every living being maintains its stability by being excitable [movable] and able to adjust itself to respond to any movement. It is stable because it is modifiable.' Apply this principle to the life of Jesus, and what do we find? When something unpleasant or difficult happened to Him, He felt keenly the catastrophic nature of the thing that had occurred, but on each occasion, because of His inner strength and calm, was able to adjust. If He had been incapable of feeling disturbed (yet without sinning) then He could not have identified with us in our human predicament.

Disruption comes to us all. The question is not whether or not it will trouble us, but how quickly we are able to make the adjustment from disruption to inner strength and calm. Many take a long time to adjust; the period of disruption is protracted, the suffering drawn out until the person concerned becomes devastated. Christ can so brand us with His spirit of inner strength and peace, however, that we adjust more quickly to life's disruptions and make shorter our hours of hesitation.

Father, I do not ask to be exempt from the ordinary trials and disruptions that life may bring me, but I do ask for help to adjust more rapidly - to pass as quickly as possible from the troubled mind to the tranquil mind. Amen.

Woman to **Woman**

Paula Buchel, tells us about her first experience of the **Woman to Woman** course, CWR's flagship course for women who want to help and minister to other women.

Paula Buchel,
Women's Ministry tutor,
until June 2014

I went on the course at a key time in my life. I had just been made redundant and was embarking on a change of career. The thirty women on the course with me were a great mix of ages and backgrounds. Over the five days together we grew close and supportive of one another. I was able to spend time with them, time alone and time with God.

It was an intense period of learning about God's plan for my life and gaining a better understanding of the person I was. It was as if God warmed me up during that week to the idea that He was leading me into working with women. By the end of the week I felt He had challenged me to be ready to step out more confidently for Him.

The week inspired me, filled me spiritually, sharpened my awareness of that 'still small voice', and encouraged me at a time when I really needed it. As I write, I am preparing to return to South Africa, but I know my experience at CWR will prove invaluable in the future.

The next course takes place **13–17 October 2014** at Waverley Abbey House. For full course details, or to book, call **+44 (0)1252 784719** or visit **www.cwr.org.uk/women**

What strength - what calm!

FOR READING & MEDITATION - ACTS 6:8-15

'they could not stand up against his wisdom or the Spirit by whom he spoke.' (v10)

For one more day we consider the need to be branded with the mark of inner strength and calm. The question arises: Can the inner strength and calm Jesus so clearly demonstrated in His life be made available to us? Open your New Testament and what do you discover? On almost every page you find instances of His early disciples – especially after Pentecost – remaining inwardly steady in all kinds of situations, full of inner strength and calm.

Take, for example, the first Christian martyr – Stephen. When he was dragged before the Sanhedrin (the Jewish religious council) and lies were told about him, we read that 'his face was like the face of an angel' (v15). The lies were turned to light. And when they stoned him, he knelt down amid the shower of stones and prayed: '"Lord, do not hold this sin against them"' (Acts 7:60). This is inner strength – and peace.

FURTHER STUDY

Jer. 17:7-8;
Dan. 6:6-16

1. What overcomes fear and worry?

2. How did Daniel's routine remain undisturbed in danger?

Take another illustration – that of the great apostle Paul. The ship is about to go to pieces beneath him, and he stands and says: 'Keep up your courage, men, for I have faith in God' (Acts 27:25). After that, Paul, though a prisoner, takes charge of the ship, tells the soldiers guarding him what to do and saves himself and the whole company. What inner strength – what calm!

The same spirit which had lived in Jesus was now working in His disciples. And if He lived in them, then surely He can live in us. Time has not eroded Christ's ability to communicate to His followers the strength and peace which characterised His own ministry while here on earth. What He was, He is, and what He was and is, He always will be.

Blessed Lord and Master, stamp this mark of Yours - the mark of inner strength and peace - into my flesh, my blood and my nerve tissue, so that never again shall life's disasters leave me a wreck. For Your own dear name's sake. Amen.

Afraid of sanity?

FOR READING & MEDITATION - LUKE 8:26-39

'they found the man from whom the demons had gone out, sitting at Jesus' feet ... and they were afraid.' (v35)

It is time now to examine yet another characteristic of Christ which we can have branded into our lives – the ability to look for the good in even difficult circumstances. When bad things happened in the life of Jesus, He did not whine or complain but faced up to everything that occurred and viewed it through the perspective of the bigger story of God.

In the passage we have read today we see how, after Jesus had healed the demon-possessed man, the people came and saw the man 'sitting ... dressed and in his right mind'. Then come the words: 'And they were afraid.' Afraid? Intriguing. What were they afraid of? Afraid of sanity? They couldn't understand how the miracles occurred so they became fearful and they 'asked him to depart from them' (v37, RSV). How would you feel, I wonder, if the non-Christians in your community signed a petition to ask you and your church to move elsewhere? Would you feel that your ministry and service for Jesus were being blocked? Then take note of this: providing you are in close fellowship with Jesus, nothing and no one can block your service for God. Difficulties did not frustrate Jesus, and they need not frustrate you.

FURTHER STUDY

Acts 16:6-15; Rom. 8:28

1. What happened when Paul's plans were blocked?

2. What is our conviction?

One Bible commentator highlights that after being asked to leave Gadara, Jesus performed some of His most wonderful miracles. For instance, He raised a dead girl to life, and fed the 5,000. What is more, He taught some of the greatest truths. Jesus refused to let difficulties overcome Him. You and I need to be branded with this same spirit – the attitude of faith that is undeterred by difficulties but rather looks for the good.

O God my Father, brand within me the conviction that I need not be deterred by petty or even decisive blocking of my plans. If there is no way through then with You I can find a way around. Thank You, Father. Amen.

When plans are interrupted

FOR READING & MEDITATION – MATTHEW 14:13-21

'When Jesus landed and saw a large crowd, he had compassion on them and healed their sick.' (v14)

We saw yesterday how, after being blocked from ministering in the district of Gadara, Jesus went on to do some of the greatest things of His life. The blocking became a blessing! It is true that sometimes it is disconcerting – and to some discouraging – to find one's best endeavours blocked by misunderstanding and self-interest. But was Jesus blocked by these? No; He simply turned in another direction – temporarily deterred, but not deflected.

A social worker in a newspaper report commented: 'One of the reasons why there is such an increase in drug-taking is because people find it increasingly difficult to deal with frustration.' Do you know how to handle frustration? Jesus did – when frustrating things happened to Him, He knew to look for the good that could come out of them.

Look again at the picture which is painted for us in today's passage. Jesus had just heard that John the Baptist, His cousin and forerunner, had been put to death. The account says: 'When Jesus got the news, he slipped away by boat to an out-of-the-way place by himself' (v13, *The Message*). He wanted to be alone to work through the grief which came upon Him after hearing of John's death. But what happened then? 'Soon a lot of people from the nearby villages walked around the lake to where he was' (v13, *The Message*). They interrupted His plans. How did Jesus respond to this? With frustration? With anger? No – He used the situation for good, healing the sick and miraculously feeding the multitude. When His plans were hampered, He simply made bigger ones. So can we.

FURTHER STUDY

Acts 16:19-34; Phil. 1:12-14

1. How did the apostles' block turn to blessing?

2. How did Paul's imprisonment further Christ's cause?

Lord Jesus, stamp into my being the conviction that when I am powerless to change my situation, I can change my outlook. And through that changed outlook I can turn the blocks into blessings. Amen.

Responding in love

FOR READING & MEDITATION - LUKE 10:25-37

'On one occasion an expert in the law stood up to test Jesus.' (v25)

Today we examine more examples of the way in which Jesus took a moment of frustration in His ministry and turned it into an occasion of fruitfulness. An expert of the law 'stood up to put him to the test' (v25, RSV). Notice that. This was not an innocent approach, but an insidious one.

There can be little doubt that the law expert's intention was to discredit the Son of God, but Jesus took his question about the Law and used it to reveal something beyond Moses' Law – the law of love. Jesus answered him in words that have lived on through the centuries – the unforgettable story of the Good Samaritan. You and I might have responded to the expert's question with a certain amount of pique, but not Jesus. He responded to every situation in love.

His reaction when the Pharisees complained that He 'receives sinners and eats with them' (Luke 15:2, RSV) was to tell them a group of parables: the parable of the lost sheep, the parable of the lost coin and parable of the lost son – all revelations of the seeking, redemptive God. What a response to an accusation!

Think again of the moment when Jesus was nailed to the cross. Life seemed to have acted with terrifying severity against Him: He was betrayed, denied, humiliated, forsaken, crucified, spat upon, afflicted. What was His response? 'Father, forgive them, for they do not know what they are doing' (Luke 23:34) – the highest reaction ever witnessed on this planet. In the words of one commentator: 'All His reactions were revelations.' May they impact us and teach us how we can respond to others.

FURTHER STUDY

Luke 20:20-26; John 8:1-11

1. How did Jesus use a trap to teach?

2. How did Jesus turn yet another test into a revelation of mercy?

Father, I am grateful that Scripture has recorded so many of Your Son's loving responses. Grant me the ability to react in a similar way to all things - not in self-pity but with the same heart of love. Amen.

Satan has no power

FOR READING & MEDITATION - JOHN 14:15-31

'the ruler of this world ... has no power over me; but I do as the Father has commanded me' (vv30-31, RSV)

The characteristic of Jesus about which we are thinking is that of being able to view difficult situations with God's perspective. In today's text we see that, even though Jesus was using this final time with His disciples to try to prepare them, and even though He must have felt heavy in His spirit because of what was about to happen (shown in the Garden of Gethsemane soon after), He still indicated that what Satan intended for evil – to crush Him once and for all – would actually be the way God saved the world.

FURTHER STUDY

Eph. 4:25-32;
1 John 5:1-5

1. How can we avoid giving Satan a foothold?

2. How can we overcome in all things?

How was Jesus able to view it like that, and how can we? Make sure that Satan has no hold on you. Jesus was able to say that Satan had no power over Him – and so can you. He knew that Satan's most determined efforts would contribute to divine ends. And so can you if you make sure that there is nothing in you which the devil can hold over you, such as self-pity, self-centredness, resentment, inferiority or any other kind of sin.

Paul, when writing to the Corinthians on the importance of forgiveness, reminded them that a forgiving spirit would prevent Satan from getting a foothold in their lives: 'To keep Satan from gaining the advantage over us; for we are not ignorant of his designs' (2 Cor. 2:11, RSV). When we take the trouble to remove all roots of bitterness, all those things which are displeasing to Christ from our lives, then, by God's grace, we ensure that Satan cannot gain a foothold. Knowing he has no power, we can look for the ways in which God will use his schemes for good.

O Father, I know that You are both ready and willing to brand Your characteristics into my life, but today I see that there is something I must do too. Help me to put away every known sin this day. In Jesus' name I pray. Amen.

Kicked - forward!

FOR READING & MEDITATION - 2 CORINTHIANS 12:1-10

'for Christ's sake, I delight in weaknesses, in insults, in hardships ...
For when I am weak, then I am strong.' (v10)

The question that inevitably arises as we meditate on the marks of Jesus is this: How deeply can we expect these characteristics of Jesus to be branded into us? The answer is: to the same degree that we are willing to give ourselves to Him.

Apart from Jesus, the other person in the New Testament who clearly looked for the good in every situation, even though he faced some horrendous trials, was the apostle Paul. The marks of Jesus, as we said, were not only branded into his flesh but into the very texture of his being. Consider today's example. When Paul asked God to take away the 'thorn in the flesh' – the 'messenger of Satan' that harassed him – he received the reply: 'My grace is sufficient for you, for my power is made perfect in weakness.' He was promised, not deliverance, but power to use the infirmity. His response? 'Therefore I will boast all the more gladly about my weaknesses ... For when I am weak, then I am strong.'

Dr E. Stanley Jones said of this passage: 'If the messenger of Satan was to buffet him, then he would determine the direction in which the blows would send him.' And which way did they send him? Forward! Some time ago, as I got into the back seat of a friend's car, the front-seat passenger remarked: 'My seat needs to come forward a little, but it seems to be stuck. Kick it forward!' I obliged, and as I did so I reminded myself that this is precisely what life does to one who is branded with the characteristics of Jesus. Life may kick him, but he determines the direction in which he goes after he is kicked – forward.

FURTHER STUDY

John 2:1-10;
1 Cor. 4:11-16

1. Was Jesus annoyed or kicked forward by Mary?

2. How can we imitate Paul?

O Father, just as You branded into Paul the ability to see the good in every situation, brand me with that same ability, I pray. Abide with me, and then I can abide everything. And not just abide it – but use it. Amen.

Impediments need not impede

FOR READING & MEDITATION - GALATIANS 4:1-14

'As you know, it was because of an illness that I first preached the gospel to you.' (v13)

Today we continue looking at the way in which the apostle Paul, one of Jesus' most devoted followers, used all situations and circumstances for good. Our text tells us that when Paul first came to Galatia he was suffering from an illness, and this affliction caused him to stay with the Galatians and preach the gospel to them. *The Message* translates Paul's words in this way: 'You were well aware that the reason I ended up preaching to you was that I was physically broken.'

In checking this with a number of commentaries, I note

FURTHER STUDY

Mark 6:1-6;
John 1:44-46;
1 Tim. 4:9-16

1. What impediments did Jesus overcome?

2. Why might people have looked down on Timothy?

that there seems to be some uncertainty regarding this illness. The words may refer to a physical weakness from which Paul suffered constantly or to an illness such as malaria. Whatever the illness, it caused Paul to travel to Galatia in search of a climate that would be beneficial to him. What we do know is that he did not allow his condition to frustrate him. Forced by the illness to spend time in Galatia, he turned those circumstances for good and started to evangelise in the province. Later he wrote a letter to the churches which had been established there – a letter which has enriched the Church for close on 2,000 years. And it will go on enriching it until the end of time. At another time in his life Paul made this admission: 'I may not be a trained speaker' (2 Cor. 11:6). But did that stop his ministry? Most certainly not. He took up his pen and gave the world the letters that are among the greatest writings of history. He made every kick send him forward – and learned how to function where his usefulness really mattered.

O Father, give me the same intentionality over circumstances that Jesus and Paul so clearly demonstrated. Help me to see that I am not beaten until I am beaten within. And if You are with me I may be shaken but need never be shattered. Amen.

Will you **Pay it Forward**?

Next year we celebrate CWR's 50th anniversary, and as part of the celebrations we're focusing on where it all started – daily Bible reading notes.

When he began writing *Every Day with Jesus* on the back of postcards for his church, Selwyn Hughes recognised that our devotional times with God are the cornerstone of our on-going walk on this journey of faith.

PLAYING YOUR PART

We're still passionate about reading God's Word, and want to encourage as many people as possible to engage with His Word on a daily basis. So if you have been blessed by reading *Every Day with Jesus*, *Inspiring Women Every Day*, *Cover to Cover Every Day*, *Life Every Day*, *Mettle*, *YP's* or *Topz* then we would love you to **pay the blessing forward** by giving someone a copy or gift subscription of our dated Bible reading notes.

Keep an eye open in the coming months for more information on how you can get involved and **Pay it Forward** in 2015. You can also find out more information online – just visit **www.cwr.org.uk/payitforward**

'No Wailing Wall'

FOR READING & MEDITATION - HOSEA 2:1-20

'There I will give her back her vineyards, and will make the Valley of Achor a door of hope.' (v15)

Long before Christ came into the world, Hosea saw that God is the One who has the resources to turn all the bad things that happen to us to advantage: 'I'll turn Heartbreak Valley into Acres of Hope' (v15, *The Message*). How thrilling.

As I was about to begin this page, my eye fell upon a statement which gave me a new direction: 'There is no "Wailing Wall" in the Christian Church.' The writer was referring, of course, to the fact that in Jerusalem thousands of Jews visit the remains of Solomon's Temple – the Western Wall – and there pray for their personal needs and the restoration of the Temple. It has come to be known as the 'Wailing Wall' because of the anguish that is poured out before those ancient stones. Christianity, however, has no such place. The place where Christians congregate and linger when they visit Jerusalem is not the Wailing Wall but the open tomb.

FURTHER STUDY

1 John 4:1-6;
Rev. 5:1-9

1. Why can we overcome all things that are against us?

2. Why do we no longer need to weep?

That's one difference between Christianity and Judaism. One stops at a Wailing Wall, the other starts at an open tomb. When neighbours saw Mary of Bethany leave the house, they supposed she was going to the tomb of Lazarus: 'They imagined she was going to wail at the tomb' (John 11:31, Moffatt). They could think of nothing to be done except to wail at a tomb. But Mary did not go to wail at the tomb; she went to speak to a Person. And what had He told her sister? 'I am the resurrection and the life' (John 11:25). He was the answer. He still is. The inner strength He had to take whatever came and use it can be branded into you. What a way to live!

Gracious Father, I await Your branding so that never again will I complain or sulk when things do not go my way. Instead, I will take everything that comes and use it. Brand me now, dear Father - now. In Jesus' name. Amen.

Christ's supreme loyalty

FOR READING & MEDITATION - JOHN 6:25-40

'For I have come down from heaven not to do my will but to do the will of him who sent me.' (v38)

As we continue meditating on the thought that we are to be branded with the marks of Jesus, we turn our attention to another characteristic of Christ which we need to have stamped into us – single-mindedness, which is best described as focused determination.

Even the most casual reader of the Gospels cannot help but notice that Jesus was an utterly focused and resolute person. The first glimpse of this characteristic is provided by the words He spoke to His mother in the Temple when just 12: 'Did you not see and know that it is necessary [as a duty] for Me to be in My Father's house and [occupied] about My Father's business?' (Luke 2:49, Amplified Bible). After launching into His public ministry, aged 30, He spoke often of the mission which lay before Him, namely the cross. It is quite clear, also, that He allowed nothing to divert Him from this purpose. As He strides through the pages of the Gospels He appears to have one thing uppermost in His mind: fulfilling His Father's will.

You and I are not likely to be called to die upon a cross, but we are called to do the Father's will, so the characteristic of absolute focus which Christ so wonderfully displayed can be infused into us, too. Are you committed to pursuing God's individual plans for your life wholeheartedly? Can you travel on undeterred when self-interests thrust their tantalising appeal before your path? Every one of us, I am sure – myself included – needs this characteristic to be branded more deeply into us so that we will not be delayed or diverted from pursuing the path set out by our Father's will.

FURTHER STUDY

Heb. 10:1-10

1. What was the result of Jesus' single-minded purpose?

2. How can such single-mindedness overcome self-interest?

Blessed Lord Jesus, You who set Your face to go to the cross without wavering, give me that same decisive attitude of mind. Let me resolve with all my being to do Your will. Amen.

Waiting – yet wanting

FOR READING & MEDITATION - MATTHEW 20:20-28

'Then the mother of Zebedee's sons came to Jesus with her sons
and ... asked a favour of him.' (v20)

Yesterday we started to consider another brand mark of
Jesus which needs to become part of our personalities
– focused determination. As you go about your business
this day, pause for a moment and ask yourself these
questions: Am I a resolutely focused person? Do I allow
myself to be deterred from doing what I know is God's
will? How committed am I to pursuing God's individual
plan for my life?

The whole issue of single-mindedness can be seen in a
clearer light when we place it against its opposite – double-
mindedness. Double-mindedness, as far as the
Christian life is concerned, consists of pursuing
two different purposes at one and the same time
– God's purpose and your purpose. I can't be sure
about this, but it seems to me that the mother of
James and John was a double-minded person. In
Matthew 27:55–56 we read that she was one of
the women who 'had followed Jesus from Galilee
to care for his needs'. The Moffatt translation says
that these women 'waited on him'. Yet, despite
waiting on Him, she wanted something for her
two sons – seats to the right and left of Jesus in
His kingdom.

**FURTHER
STUDY**

Matt. 4:1-10;
John 12:1-6

1. How did
Jesus' single-
mindedness
overcome
temptation?

2. How was
Judas double-
minded?

I don't want to be too hard on this mother
because I recognise that not enough is said to give an
accurate picture of her, but I do wonder if her ministry
to Jesus was somewhat spoiled by ulterior motives. Did
she want to use the kingdom for purposes of prestige for
her two sons? Although I cannot be sure, I am sure about
the tendency in my own heart to use spiritual means for
selfish ends. Perhaps you have noticed a similar tendency
in your heart also. If so, then join me in this prayer:

**Lord Jesus, You whose motives and acts were pure and
whose impact upon life changed the world, give me that same
singleness of motive that I, too, may change my little world – for
You. For Your own dear name's sake. Amen.**

Dear friend,

We thank God and all of you who have enabled this ministry to flourish, grow and **touch millions of lives** around the world over the past 50 years.

It never ceases to amaze me how many testimonies come in from all over the world, such as a recent invitation to a young man's baptism in prison. Through the free publications we make available via prison chaplains, he has given his life to Christ and taken the first steps in his newfound faith.

A rich heritage

In 1965 ... Selwyn Hughes established CWR with a desire to see the church grow in the knowledge and understanding of God through prayer and daily engagement with His Word, fanning the flames of personal and national **transformation and revival**.

In 1987 ... CWR moved into Waverley Abbey House, from which many thousands of lives have been changed and continue to benefit richly from **hearing and applying** the Word of God.

In 2006 ... Selwyn went to be with the Lord, his whole life and ministry having been an **investment** which enabled him to become part of something far bigger than himself, and that lives on today. Just like the small boy who offered up his loaves and fishes to Jesus, God has been able to multiply the effect of Selwyn's offering, transforming lives around the world.

WAVERLEY ABBEY
COLLEGE

In 2012 ... God opened the door for much needed space and expansion by providing CWR with Pilgrim Hall. Since that time we have established **Waverley Abbey College** whose initiatives in counselling and education continue to gain momentum, equipping godly men and women to be people of influence in their chosen vocations and professions.

In 2014 ... God has enabled CWR, through the generosity of a significant loan, **to purchase Annan Court**, a conference facility *adjacent* to Pilgrim Hall! Through **God's grace** and timing, the chance to reunite these two sites was an immediate, unexpected and exciting opportunity which will house the growing initiatives from Waverley Abbey College.

So we find ourselves, poised on the brink of our 50th year, with the opportunity to secure the future of the ministry and its commitment to society's changing needs for the **next 50 years**.

Today ... we need your help

Although we have taken one of our biggest **steps of faith** yet, the challenges and opportunities we face in what is considered a post-Christian era and largely biblically-illiterate culture, require us to **flex our muscles of faith** and dependency on God even further.

Whilst remaining **rooted in a rich heritage**, we are now poised to move on, with what we believe is God's leading, in several areas of our ministry for Him:

- Opportunities are opening up for us to take our teaching regionally and internationally; we are being asked for more teaching and resources especially for men, for women and for children

- We have much work to do at Annan Court (above) to update and modernise the campus
- Exciting partnership opportunities to equip more people to realise their God-given potential

Will you, like Selwyn, invest now in a legacy for the future?

Invest in spreading the Word

A legacy in life transforming initiatives to engage, hear, read, understand and apply God's Word to everyday life and relationships.

Invest in helping others

A legacy in helping people make good and godly choices, enabling a confidence in and a daily reliance on the scriptures.

Invest for the future

A legacy in the lives of those who will be touched by the ministry in the coming years. People who will then be equipped to serve in their place of calling to work for God.

May I thank you in advance for your generosity on behalf of all those in whose lives you are investing, for helping them to bind up the broken-hearted and proclaim freedom for the captives.

Grace and peace,

Mick Brooks, CWR Chief Executive

Yes,

I want to invest in spreading the Word, helping others and join you in this step of faith.

Gift amount: ☐ £50 ☐ £100 ☐ £200 ☐ £500

£_____ Preferred amount

Or to donate online go to **www.cwr.org.uk/stepoffaith**

☐ Please send me an acknowledgement of my gift.

YOUR DETAILS (REQUIRED FOR ORDERS AND DONATIONS)

Name: CWR ID No. (if known):

Home Address:

Postcode:

Telephone No. (for queries):   Email:

GIFT AID (YOUR HOME ADDRESS REQUIRED, SEE ABOVE)

giftaid it

I am a UK taxpayer and want CWR to reclaim the tax on all my donations for the four years prior to this year **and on** all donations I make from the date of this Gift Aid declaration until further notice.*

Taxpayer's Full Name (in BLOCK CAPITALS) _____

Signature _____ **Date** _____

*I understand I must pay an amount of Income/Capital Gains Tax at least equal to the tax the charity reclaims in the tax year.

PAYMENT DETAILS

☐ I enclose a cheque/PO made payable to CWR for the amount of: £ _____

☐ Please charge my credit/debit card.

Cardholder's name (in BLOCK CAPITALS) _____

Card No. ☐☐☐☐ ☐☐☐☐ ☐☐☐☐ ☐☐☐☐ ☐☐☐☐

Expires end ☐☐☐☐   Security Code ☐☐☐

CWR Applying God's Word *to everyday life and relationships*

CWR, Waverley Abbey House, Waverley Lane, Farnham, Surrey GU9 8EP

CWR is a registered charity No. 294387 and a limited company registered in England No. 1990308

Once funds have been raised to meet the immediate needs of this appeal, CWR reserves the right to use any monies received to fund other Bible-based ministry around the world.

Inner division

FOR READING & MEDITATION – MATTHEW 6:19-34

'The eye is the lamp of the body. If your eyes are good, your whole body will be full of light.' (v22)

We spoke yesterday of the mother of James and John who wanted something for her two sons – places of honour beside Jesus in His kingdom.

Some time ago I heard a Christian counsellor tell how he counselled a woman who was going through a serious emotional conflict. He had discovered that the cause of her inner conflict was her desire for her daughter to marry an army officer so that she could then proudly introduce him as her son-in-law. She had convinced herself that the marriage was for her daughter's happiness, but really it was for her own benefit. There was a little more to the sad story than that, of course, but I know from my own dealings with people that double-mindedness can set up conflicts within people's lives that tip them into serious mental and physical health issues.

It was said of Amaziah: 'He did what was right in the eyes of the LORD, but not wholeheartedly' (2 Chron. 25:2). Moffatt translates the verse like this: 'He did what was right in the eyes of the Eternal, but not with an undivided mind'. Paul put his finger on the problem when he said: 'I am afraid that your minds may be seduced from a single-hearted devotion to him [Christ]' (2 Cor. 11:3, Phillips). When there is division in our thoughts, it is not long before there is division in our actions, and thereafter the division is registered in us – inevitably. A famous psychologist said: 'We must be held together by a single-minded devotion, otherwise we begin to fall to pieces.' This is how it was with Jesus – and we too can decide to be one person, with one overarching motive, moving towards one goal.

FURTHER STUDY

1 Kings 11:1-4;
2 Tim. 4:9-10

1. What was the result of Solomon's divided heart?

2. What was Demas' inner division?

My Father and my God, I see that no heart is big enough for two mutually exclusive loves. Brand in me still more deeply this mark of Jesus – to be one person, with one motive, moving towards one goal. For Jesus' sake. Amen.

'Falling-to-pieces' living

FOR READING & MEDITATION – JAMES 1:1-8

'he is a double-minded man, unstable in all he does.' (v8)

The subject on which we are meditating is focused determination, but in order to get a better understanding of the issue we are looking at the other side of the coin – double-mindedness.

Yesterday I referred to a statement made by a famous psychologist: 'We must be held together by a single-minded devotion, otherwise we begin to fall to pieces.' How true. It was said of the prodigal son that he 'wasted his fortune in reckless and loose [from restraint] living' (Luke 15:13, Amplified Bible). His 'loose-from-restraint' type of living was so loose that he fell to pieces; it could be called 'falling-to-pieces' living. His life had no inner cement, no moral fortification, no inner strength and peace. The apostle James sums up the matter in the words of today's text: 'For ... a man of two minds (hesitating, dubious, irresolute) ... is unstable and unreliable and uncertain about everything' (Amplified Bible). The inner division affects everything, making the man unstable and ineffective.

FURTHER STUDY

Mark 10:17-25;
James 4:7-8

1. How did the rich man's double-mindedness affect him?

2. What should the double-minded do?

Many years ago, a missionary told how, having docked at Shanghai, he saw a sign on a warehouse that read: 'Your baggage taken and delivered in all directions.' If we are double-minded then we end up delivering ourselves in too many directions. We need to learn, as I said yesterday, to be one person, with one motive, moving towards one goal. Archbishop William Temple once wrote: 'Conversion means cohesion.' To this we could add: 'and conservation too'. It means – depending on how much we allow Jesus to brand His nature into us – that we are no longer wasting energy and time in conflicts which cancel us out.

O Lord Jesus, infuse into the chaos of my divisions the singleness of Your purpose. May all the clamouring voices be still at the sound of Your command. From the depths of my heart I ask this. Help me, dear Lord. Amen.

Three steps to calamity

FOR READING & MEDITATION - ROMANS 7:14-25

'Who will rescue me from this body of death? Thanks be to God – through Jesus Christ our Lord!' (vv24-25)

We continue our consideration of the opposite to focused determination – double-mindedness. I am convinced that this is a factor at the root of many personality problems. Remember what we said about Amaziah two days ago? 'He did what was right in the eyes of the Eternal, but not with an undivided mind' (2 Chron. 25:2, Moffatt). This inner division was his undoing. Listen to what follows: 'Amaziah brought the gods of the men of Seir and set them up to be his gods' (2 Chron. 25:14, Moffatt). Then listen again to what is said about him later in the same chapter: 'No sooner did Amaziah cease to follow the Eternal, than a conspiracy was formed against him' (2 Chron. 25:27, Moffatt).

The steps which lead from inner division to disaster can be plotted in this way: (1) outwardly correct but inwardly divided; (2) the inner division shows itself in outer disloyalty; (3) this leads to downfall. Many writers have given expression to this problem of double-mindedness that afflicts the human heart, but none more vividly than Edward Sanford Martin, who wrote:

> *Within my earthly temple there's a crowd,*
> *There's one of us that's humble, one that's proud,*
> *There's one that's broken-hearted for his sins,*
> *And one who, unrepentant, sits and grins.*
> *There's one who loves his neighbour as himself,*
> *And one who cares for naught but fame and self.*
> *From much corroding care would I be free*
> *If once I could determine which is me.*

Each of us must be one man or woman, not two; and that one man or one woman must be God's man or God's woman.

FURTHER STUDY

1 Sam. 15:13-29

1. How would Saul's double-mindedness bring calamity?

2. Contrast Saul with what it says about the Glory of Israel.

O God, I ask You to make me one person – not two. You alone could make me, and You alone can remake me. I'm ready to be remade – from top to bottom. Do it now – today. Amen.

'I feel like a lot of pieces'

FOR READING & MEDITATION - PSALM 119:1-16

'Blessed are they who keep his statutes and seek him with all their heart.' (v2)

You probably don't need me to tell you this, but double-mindedness and inner division can be a major cause of wasted energy. A young man once stood up in a meeting and said: 'I feel like a lot of pieces of people thrown together.' His life wasn't a single entity, governed by one central purpose. We are designed by God to move towards an overall central purpose and, when we don't, we simply fail to function as we were designed to. Jotham, unlike Amaziah, to whom we have already made reference, 'grew powerful because he walked steadfastly before the LORD his God' (2 Chron. 27:6).

FURTHER STUDY

Acts 17:16-34

1. Why was the Athenians' spirituality in pieces?

2. How did they respond to Paul's call for single-mindedness?

I remember as a teenager going to my uncle, who was also my pastor, and talking with him about my intentions of going into the ministry. He told me that he detected in me some uncertainty of heart, and when I re-examined myself in the light of his insight I found that I was indeed caught up in an inner conflict. At the time I was studying engineering, and a part of me wanted to pursue this, while another part of me wanted to respond to God's call to go into the Christian ministry.

My uncle's words to me at that time have stayed with me. Now, more than five decades later, I can recall them as if they were spoken yesterday: 'Make up your mind as to what you really want – and then give yourself to that with all of your heart.' There and then I made up my mind to follow the call to the ministry, surrendered my love of mechanical engineering to the Lord, and instead received a greater love – a love for people. Since then my lifelong objective has been to serve God and help people – hence *Every Day with Jesus.*

O Father, take all my conflicting motives and bring them under one control - Your control. And whatever path You have for me to follow, help me not to love things more than people. For Jesus' sake. Amen.

Decision day

FOR READING & MEDITATION – PHILIPPIANS 3:1-14

'Forgetting what is behind and straining towards what is ahead, I
press on towards the goal' (vv13-14)

On this, our last day of looking together at the subject of
focused determination (and also its opposite – double-
mindedness), it is time to make a clear decision. Because
we are designed by God to function best when we have
a central objective and goal, we can give ourselves to
God's individual will for our lives with absolute devotion.
Anything less than this and life becomes divided – hence
disrupted. So right now, I am going to ask you to take three
simple steps.

(1) Surrender your divided self into God's hands so that
He has you. Notice that I say 'you'. Not merely
this thing or that thing – but you. When this
happens, you are no longer in your own hands,
but in His hands – He has you. (2) Commit
yourself to finding out what God wants you to
do, and to making the pursuit of His will the one
overall objective of your life. The will of God is the
only thing that is capable of holding you together
as a person. Decide right now that you will be
completely committed in doing God's will.

(3) Ask Him to fill and flow through you with
His Holy Spirit so that the inner depths of your
being are brought into unity. Tell God that you
don't want to be like those people who 'proclaim
Christ for their own ends' (Phil. 1:17, Moffatt). Let
Him know that you long to be as resolutely focused as
Christ was, and that you want that same characteristic
to be imprinted on you. As you ask, so shall you receive
– single-mindedness will be branded into you. Whenever
you feel you are starting to be torn and disrupted by
double-mindedness take it to God and place your life in His
hands once again.

**FURTHER
STUDY**

Rom. 8:5-8;
12:1-2;
Phil. 3:17-21

1. How can our
minds have a
single godly
purpose?

2. Why is our
mind and
attitude so
important?

**Gracious Father, once and for all brand this mark of Jesus into
the deepest parts of my being so that never again will my life be
held back by double-mindedness. For Your own dear name's sake
I ask it. Amen.**

'Never in a hurry'

FOR READING & MEDITATION - JOHN 11:1-16

'Yet when he heard that Lazarus was sick, he stayed where he was two more days.' (v6)

Now we start to consider another mark of Jesus – the skilled and thoughtful way in which He managed His time. No one has ever used time as effectively as Jesus. He seemed to achieve so much during the three and a half years of His public ministry, yet wherever we meet Him in the Gospels, He never appears to be in haste. What does that say to us? It's not so much the hours you put in that count – but what you put into the hours.

One writer said that in his studies of the life of Christ he was struck by three characteristics he showed in his everyday life: 'Jesus never worried, never hurried and was never flurried'. When Jesus told His disciples that He intended to return to Judea, they pleaded with Him to change His mind, giving as their reason: 'Rabbi, the Jews only recently were intending and trying to stone You, and are You [thinking of] going back there again?' (John 11:8, Amplified Bible). Christ's reply to that question was this: 'Are there not twelve hours in the day? If anyone walks in the day, he does not stumble, because he sees the light of this world' (v9, NASB).

FURTHER STUDY

2 Sam. 18:19-23;
John 9:1-7

1. Why did Ahimaaz waste his time?

2. What did Jesus explain?

It was as if Jesus was saying: 'It is not a question of what they will or will not do – there are 12 hours in the day, and I must take advantage of them to fulfil the task which God has given me to do regardless of the consequences.'

Jesus knew that the day was for His mission and the night for rest – and made full use of both. And His redemptive mission would be carried on despite the obstacles that confronted Him. We, too, can be branded with this mark of Jesus – the effective use of time.

Lord Jesus, when I look at You I see that, although You were never in a hurry, You always had time for the priorities of the day – and I long to make this my own practice too. Help me, Lord. Amen.

Time – a trust, not a tyranny

FOR READING & MEDITATION – JOHN 7:1-14

'I am not yet going up to this Feast, because for me the right time has not yet come.' (v8)

Yesterday we made the comment that whenever we look at Jesus in the Gospels, He appears never to be in haste. There was nothing fussy or frenetic about His life; He was always in charge of time – time was never in charge of Him. Being in charge of time means that you are not threatened or intimidated by it. Charles E. Hummel, in the booklet he wrote entitled *The Tyranny of the Urgent* said: 'We are not to be tyrannised by time … but trustees of it.' How do you see time? As your master – or as your servant?

Jesus was not only a good steward of His time but He was also deeply sensitive to the matter of timing. To use time well one has to know when to get up and go, and when to wait or stay behind. In the passage before us today we find a perfect example of Christ's sense of timing, for when His brothers urged Him to go to the Feast of Tabernacles in Judea so that more people might see His miracles, He knew it was not His time so stuck to His decision not to go.

FURTHER STUDY

Eccl. 3:1-8;
Gal. 4:1-5

1. What does the teacher explain?

2. When did Jesus come to earth?

Jesus' sense of time, and also His sense of timing, can be branded into us so that we can live our lives as He intended. Theologians in former days used to talk about the stewardship of treasure, time and talent. Not everyone has the same amount of treasure and talent, but everyone has the same amount of time. You have 24 hours in your day, just as I have in mine. We are advised to use time wisely: 'Look carefully then how you walk, not as unwise men but as wise, making the most of the time, because the days are evil' (Eph. 5:15-16, RSV).

My Father and my God, I recognise that the time You have given me is to be a trust, not a tyranny. Help me to manage my time, for if I don't then time will manage me. In Jesus' name I pray. Amen.

Making Disciples:
How did Jesus do it?

SHARING CHRIST WITH THE WORLD

At the heart of CWR's ministry, for nearly 50 years, has been the desire to inspire and encourage personal revival, discipleship and pastoral care in our churches. But making disciples has become a real challenge for churches and individuals, and is a topic that has absorbed the hearts and minds of many. Our hope as we look towards 2015 is to keep the subject of discipleship high on the Church's agenda, by offering forums to engage with the many different obstacles faced by the twenty-first century Church.

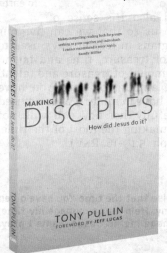

Earlier this year we released the book *Making Disciples: How did Jesus do it?* by Tony Pullin. The book attracted strong endorsements from a diverse range of Christian leaders including Sandy Millar, Stuart Bell, Mark Bailey and Steve Clifford. Such a response reinforced to us the significance of discipleship to the Church today.

COME AND JOIN US IN 2015

As a result, we are looking to work further with Tony in offering four or five regional forums during spring 2015. Each forum will consist of local and national speakers who will contribute their own perspective, reflecting their particular strengths and experience. Time will also be included for discussion, reflection and prayer.

We hope each forum will engage entire church communities, from younger Christians to church leaders, as we look closer at Jesus' last command to His followers, to 'go and make disciples'.

As Tony says in the introduction to his book, *'True discipleship has enormous potential. As always, taking Jesus' words seriously is dangerous and rewarding at the same time. But the Great Commission, still relevant to the twenty-first century, fireworks and all, remains a major key to the advance of God's kingdom.'*

TONY PULLIN

BE INVOLVED

If you would like to find out more and join us on this exciting journey during 2015, just go online to **www.cwr.org.uk/makingdisciples** or call us on **01252 784719**

taking Jesus' words seriously is dangerous and rewarding at the same time

How the branding takes place

FOR READING & MEDITATION - ROMANS 8:18-30

'For those God foreknew he also predestined to be conformed to the likeness of his Son' (v29)

The question we face today is this: If we are to have Jesus' keen appreciation of time branded into us, how is this to take place? Do we just wait before God, like a sheep when it is about to be branded, and trust Him to burn into us a greater understanding of the importance of time? Is it something that is supernaturally given without any effort on our part? No! First we recognise our deficiencies, and then ask God's help in overcoming them. This means, of course, that all transformation and change is a combination of your willingness and His amazing grace.

FURTHER STUDY

Luke 5:15-16;
John 4:27-33,39-42

1. How can we be like Jesus in our use of time?

2. Why might we miss meals?

Assuming that you are willing to sit at the feet of Jesus and learn how to manage time as He managed it, here are a few practical steps you can take. First, spend a few weeks going through the Gospels with the main goal of observing how Jesus used His time. Take one Gospel a week, if you can, and make a note of any references that are related to the way He managed time.

As an example of what I have in mind, think back to the occasion we looked at a couple of days ago, recorded in John 11, when Jesus heard of Lazarus' sickness. The account says: 'When he heard that Lazarus was sick, he stayed where he was two more days' (John 11:6). Why did Jesus not rush to Lazarus' bedside and make him well? Because it was not the right time. Had Jesus allowed Himself to be pressured by the situation and circumstance rather than seek to understand God's mind in the matter then probably all that would have been recorded in John 11 would have been the story of Lazarus being healed. Instead, we have a miracle of resurrection!

O Father, help me to model my life, not on that of any man or woman, but on that of Your Son, the Lord Jesus Christ. Illuminate the Scriptures to me yet again as I study them day by day. For Your own dear name's sake. Amen.

Establishing priorities

FOR READING & MEDITATION - EPHESIANS 5:8-20

'making the most of the time, because the days are evil. (v16, RSV)

Yesterday we said that one of the first steps we take in improving our understanding of the importance of time – and timing – is to go through the Gospels and watch how Jesus used His days. He neither wasted time nor did He ask for more time. Jesus knew He had all the time He needed to do the work that God had committed into His hands. And so, my friend, do you.

A counsellee of mine who, at my suggestion, went through the Gospels to discover how Jesus managed His time, told me that it was one of the turning points in his life. Instead of being tyrannised by time he learned how to become a trustee of it. Dr David Seamands, an author, said: 'The biggest issue in discipleship revolves around the question: what do I do with my time?' How true.

A second step we can take in learning how to manage time is this: pray and ask God to show you how to establish your priorities in life. Also, make a list of these priorities in order of importance. I do this every now and again, and what surprises me is how, from year to year, some of the priorities remain the same while others change. Top of my list is time with God and my family – next is the writing of *Every Day with Jesus*. These priorities do not change from year to year, but some other priorities do. A priority this month may not be a priority next month. All priorities need to be examined regularly, and some might have to be brought higher up the list or put lower down the list. Even those who usually make good use of time need to occasionally check their priorities. Trusteeship demands it.

FURTHER STUDY

Luke 10:38-42; 14:16-24

1. What were the differing priorities of Mary and Martha?

2. How can wrong priorities cause us to miss God's blessing?

O Father, help me as I set about this task of establishing the priorities in my life. Give me wisdom and understanding to list things in the right order - Your order. For Jesus' sake. Amen.

Planning ahead

FOR READING & MEDITATION - 1 CORINTHIANS 9:16-27
'Run in such a way as to get the prize.' (v24)

The matter we are considering at the moment is how to view time differently – as our servant, not a tyrant. Before we leave yesterday's thought about needing to establish priorities, let me add a final word about what happens when we spend time on the wrong things. After their return from captivity, the Israelites put off rebuilding God's Temple in order to construct luxurious homes for themselves. To regain their attention, the Lord withheld His blessing. 'You have planted much, but have harvested little. You eat, but never have enough. You drink, but never have your fill ... You earn wages, only to put them in a purse with holes in it' (Hag. 1:6). If you have been setting the wrong priorities, perhaps God is waiting patiently for you, allowing circumstances to get your attention.

FURTHER STUDY

1 Chron. 28:11-19;
Hag. 1:2-3

1. How did God help David plan?

2. Why did the people have wrong priorities?

A third step we can take is: learn how to plan ahead. You have probably heard the saying: 'People don't plan to fail – they fail because they don't plan.' Paul says that to win in life, we must have a purpose. 'I do not run like a man running aimlessly; I do not fight like a man beating the air' (v26). Sprinters don't line up in their starting blocks, take off at the sound of the gun, then stop to look for the finishing line. They know exactly where that finishing line is before they start and go straight for it. Paul advocated thinking ahead, as today's reading so clearly states.

Have you ever asked God to show you what He wants you to accomplish in your lifetime? If you don't know what it is, then ask, otherwise you could find your life will be like the sand dunes – drifting whichever way the wind blows.

My Father and my God, I want to be ready for the moment of my highest use, some great moment that shall call for my best. Help me, day by day, to prepare myself for that supreme moment. In Jesus' name. Amen.

Proper motivation

FOR READING & MEDITATION - MATTHEW 7:7-14

'Ask and it will be given to you; seek and you will find; knock and the door will be opened to you.' (v7)

The fourth step we can take in learning how to make best use of our time is to draw up schedules and follow them as closely as possible. Impressive plans and schedules are useless unless they are implemented. Paul, in 2 Corinthians 8, admonishes the church at Corinth for not completing a fund-raising project: 'So here's what I think: The best thing you can do right now is to finish what you started last year and not let those good intentions grow stale' (v10, *The Message*).

One key to following schedules is proper motivation. But how do we become motivated? 'That energy is God's energy, an energy deep within you, God himself willing and working at what will give him the most pleasure' (Phil. 2:13, *The Message*). God can change your desires. Ask Him – then let Him. Some time ago it occurred to me that my days would be a lot more interesting if I did only what I enjoyed doing. I could either become unreliable in activities I didn't like, or to learn to like them. That's when Philippians 2:13 hit me! God showed me that He could transform my dislikes into likes. I just needed to ask Him, then trust Him to bring it about. He did.

A fifth step in managing our time is this: learn how to make the most of your time – accomplishing as much as you can with each activity, and doing it in the best possible way. Pray and think about what you are doing, how you are doing it – and why. Is it effective in helping you accomplish an important goal? If not, modify it or stop doing it. As a steward and a trustee of God's time, He wants to help you make the most of it. Do you?

Father, I wince when You confront me like this, but I know I am being brought to one of life's clear choices. Help me to be a good steward, not only of my talents and my treasure, but also of my time. Amen.

'No unemployment'

FOR READING & MEDITATION - ECCLESIASTES 3:1-14

'That everyone may eat and drink, and find satisfaction in all his toil - this is the gift of God.' (v13)

For one last day we meditate on this issue of managing our most important resource: time. A sixth suggestion is one that I have borrowed from John Wesley, that master of the use of time: 'Never be under-employed – and never be triflingly employed.'

As God's people, we always have a job to do and we need to ensure we do it to the best of our ability, not wasting any time. If you see something that needs doing around you, don't assume someone else is going to do it – God might be waiting for you to!

FURTHER STUDY

Luke 2:36-38;
John 15:1-8

1. How did elderly Anna serve God?

2. What activities could you prune?

A seventh suggestion for using our time well is this: learn to say 'No' to things that are non-contributive. In photography we are told that the composition of a good picture depends not only on what you include in it, but also on what you leave out. Your capacity to say 'No' determines your capacity to say 'Yes'. You may have to say 'No' to some things in order to say 'Yes' to more important things. 'Life,' as one person has put it, 'depends upon elimination as well as assimilation.' During an interview a reporter asked an executive what was the first qualification of a business executive. He replied: 'A wastebasket'. We must be ready to discard things that do not contribute. Make the most of your God-given time by being a good steward. Start right away to implement the suggestions, and don't forget the point I made a few days ago: there is enough time to do and enjoy all that God has for you. If you find you are always running out of time, you are also in danger of burning out. Take a look again at your priorities.

Lord Jesus Christ, I see that just as You had enough time to complete the will of God for Your life when here on earth, so too have I. Help me to so live in the light of that truth.' Amen.

A positive negative

FOR READING & MEDITATION - LUKE 23:26-46

'Jesus ... said to them, "Daughters of Jerusalem, do not weep for me; weep for yourselves and for your children."' (v28)

As we meditate on the brand marks of Jesus we come to a characteristic of His which, although expressed in a negative form, is really a positive negative – no self-pity. Jesus didn't experience life as a victim but rather had confidence and trust in God. One can comb the record of His life with scrupulous care and not find a trace of self-pity anywhere in His personality. He suffered the cruellest treatment from those who hated Him – even from some who had been His friends – but not once does He show any evidence of being sorry for Himself. Even on the way to Golgotha He urged the women not to cry for Him.

There must have been many emotions raging through the heart of Jesus that day – pain, agony, apprehension and so on – but self-pity was not one of them. In the High Priest's palace, amid the sneering and abuse of the servants, He has little thought for Himself. Instead, He turns to Peter, the one who denied Him three times, and saves him with a look. In the Praetorium, when standing before Pilate, He appears to discuss His mission in the world with that air of inner strength and calm. And on the cross, He prays for those who have crucified Him, makes provision for His mother, and gives assurance to a penitent thief with the words: 'today you will be with me in paradise' (v43).

How forgivable it would have been for Jesus to become totally overcome by self-pity. But no – He was still thinking of others. You and I can draw so close to Christ that we will be able to say: 'I am no longer a victim, Jesus has set me free and I choose to put my confidence and trust in God.'

FURTHER STUDY

I Kings 19:1-18

1. Why was Elijah full of self-pity?

2. How did God correct his view of the situation?

Gracious Father, thank You for the work You are achieving in me day by day as I meditate on this theme - the marks of Jesus. May this mark be branded into me - the mark of no self-pity. In Jesus' name I pray. Amen.

'That stigma!'

FOR READING & MEDITATION – 2 SAMUEL 11:1-27

'After the time of mourning was over, David had her brought to his house, and she became his wife and bore him a son.' (v27)

Daniel L. Rowland, the preacher who was one of the leaders of the Welsh revival in the eighteenth century, said concerning the issue of self-pity: 'There was no self-pity in Christ's makeup, and there should be no self-pity in ours.'

My reaction to that statement when I first read it was this: 'Easier said than done'. But the more I examined the characteristics of self-pity and understood how shot through it is with self-serving and avoidance tactics, the more convinced I became that, however difficult and challenging the task, we must not give up until all self-pity has been eradicated from us. We are no longer victims of every whim and circumstance. We put our confidence and trust in God, putting aside all feelings of inferiority, all bids to gain pity for ourselves and have this mark of Christ infused deeply into us.

FURTHER STUDY

Acts 4:8-14;
1 Tim. 1:12-17

1. How did Peter rise above his past?

2. How did Paul acknowledge his past without self-pity?

Many years ago I talked to a girl who had just discovered that her real father was, in fact, a minister who had lost his reputation through an act of adultery. 'I shall never be able to look anyone in the face again,' she told me. 'The stigma is more than I can bear.' After sitting with her for several hours and sharing her grief, I gently drew her attention to this verse in Matthew's genealogy of Christ: 'David was the father of Solomon, whose mother had been Uriah's wife,' (Matt. 1:6). The text is quite revealing: his mother 'had been Uriah's wife'. That stigma. Yet Jesus never felt a victim of family background. The girl dried her tears, smiled, held up her head and quietly remarked: 'Then neither will I'.

O Father, I accept that since Jesus never experienced life as a victim because of His background, nor surrendered to feelings of inferiority, I must not do so either. Help me to be rid of all self-pity – now and always. Amen.

'Self-pity makes shipwreck'

FOR READING & MEDITATION - 1 THESSALONIANS 5:12-24

'give thanks in all circumstances, for this is God's will for you in Christ Jesus.' (v18)

Yesterday we took note of the fact that Jesus lived life with confidence, accepting and understanding his family background. He took the raw materials of His life and turned them into what someone has termed 'a new posterity'.

Life has given many what is often described as 'a raw deal' – a bad ancestry, deprivation of love, unpleasant home conditions. But all these things can be turned to good providing we put our trust and confidence in God. It is indeed hard to exaggerate the dangers of self-pity. The more we allow ourselves to feel it, the more dangerous it becomes. Dr W.E. Sangster put it this way: 'One of the greatest dangers that can befall any man is that he should lapse into a state of self-pity, that he should look so long and so intently at his troubles that he becomes a martyr to this most debilitating of mental disorders, and whines his way through life, constantly seeking an audience which will listen to his tale of woe.'

FURTHER STUDY

Job 3:1-16; 42:10-12

1. Describe Job's feelings.

2. When did he recover?

Just look at what self-pity accomplishes: it turns molehills into mountains, steals our courage, dabbles in doubt and distorts our picture of God. It assumes that we should spend our days on a bed of roses and finds constant occasion to suggest that God has forgotten to be gracious. Self-pity has caused thousands to make shipwreck of their lives. Some Christians I know attend church week after week without fail, but never rise to any heights of spiritual daring or positive achievement – all because they feel sorry for themselves. We must get rid of self-pity and the victim mentality before it gets rid of us.

O Father, when I see what being sorry for myself does to me, my heart cries out for full deliverance. Help me to stay free from self-pity. I bear Your brand. Amen.

THURS
16 OCT

'Life is sensitivity'

FOR READING & MEDITATION – MATTHEW 25:31-46
'I was hungry and you gave me something to eat ...
I was a stranger and you invited me in.' (v35)

Today we think further about the subject of self-pity. Some believe that those who are most prone to self-pity are those who are most sensitive. Life has been defined as 'sensitivity'. Lower life – such as plant and vegetable life – is sensitive only to itself. The higher you look on the scale of life, the wider and deeper is the degree of sensitivity you find. The highest point of sensitivity is recorded in Jesus' words: 'I was hungry' – every man's hunger was His hunger.

In a sense, the more highly sensitive we are, the higher we rise on the scale of life. Someone has pointed out that the oyster's skeleton – its shell – is on the outside, and its nervous system is on the inside. In this way, it protects itself from suffering. The oyster fastens itself to a rock and stays there while life sweeps on past it. It never develops, and never has any adventures.

FURTHER STUDY

Luke 10:25-37;
1 John 3:16-18

1. Contrast the Samaritan priest and Levite.

2. How should sensitivity express itself?

Human beings, however, are different. We have our skeleton on the inside and our nervous system on the outside. That means we are capable of great sensitivity – hence great suffering – but also great development. If we accept that 'life is sensitivity' then our degree of sensitivity indicates where we are on the scale of life. A prominent Christian man was once given a jack-in-the-box at his church's Christmas party. When he opened the present the toy jumped out and hit him in the face. He became extremely angry, lost his temper and resigned from the church. He wasn't just sensitive – he was oversensitive. And, as the old saying goes: 'An oversensitive ego makes a "small-time man".'

Lord Jesus, You who were totally sensitive, open to all the winds that blew, yet utterly unselfconscious, give me that same sensitivity so that I will be self-forgetful and healthy-minded. For Your own dear name's sake. Amen.

Virtues become vices

FOR READING & MEDITATION - 1 PETER 3:1-12

'live in harmony with one another; be sympathetic, love as brothers'
(v8)

We implied yesterday that those who are most prone to self-pity are often those who are most sensitive. Why should this be? Because sensitivity, which is the capacity for sympathy, the power to feel deeply, is often focused, not on others, but on the self.

Sensitivity is a good thing – a virtue. But, like all virtues, unguarded it can be a double weakness or vice. So, although sensitivity can help us to be kind and compassionate people, it can also be the cause of our downfall. One great writer claims that the word 'oversensitive' is a word that should never have been introduced into the dictionary. He claims that no one can be oversensitive. You can be wrongly sensitive – sensitive towards yourself – but you cannot be oversensitive. I am not sure whether I agree with his conclusion, but I do agree with his final statement: 'Sensitiveness directed outwardly toward others is the secret of a developing life, sensitiveness directed toward yourself is the cause of a disrupted life.'

To borrow again from the writings of Dr W.E. Sangster, a man who understood self-pity more than most: 'Sensitive people, unless they have been carefully taught that sensitiveness is capacity for sympathy (of which the world stands in such sore need), and that their power to feel deeply themselves is God's equipment to feel deeply with others, will be trapped into this miserable mood of complaint and whimper the days away.' William James divides people into the tough-minded and the tender-minded, and adds: 'Be tough-minded toward yourself and tender-minded toward others.'

FURTHER STUDY

Num. 11:10-15;
Mark 6:19-28

1. How did self-pity breed more self-pity?

2. How was Herod more sensitive to his reputation than John's life?

Lord Jesus Christ, pull away the adhesions of self-centred sensitivity which can cripple my inner life. Help me to be free from constant self-reference, and deepen my other-reference. Amen.

Ways out of self-pity

FOR READING & MEDITATION – ROMANS 15:1-13

'We who are strong ought ... not to please ourselves. Each of us
should please his neighbour for his good' (vv1-2)

Today we attempt to pin down the issue of self-pity
and give a workable definition. The one which I like
to use when speaking on this subject is this: 'Self-pity is
sensitivity turned selfish'. Put another way: self-pity is
produced by selfishness out of sensitivity.

What steps can we take, then, to ensure self-pity doesn't
overcome us? First, thank God for and give your sensitivity
to God. I once knew a woman, a distant relative, who was
as sensitive as an Aeolian harp on a mountain top. Her
sensitivity drove her to distraction. She attempted one thing
after another to try to direct her sensitivity – art,
music and so on. When all attempts at direction
failed, she tried to deaden it through drink. Then
she became a Christian. She surrendered her
sensitivity to God and found joy in expressing it
in ways that involved others.

Prior to his conversion Paul was, I think, a
highly sensitive person, but selfishly so. He
was sensitive to the fact that Jews seemed to be
abandoning their religion for a new one. After his
surrender to Christ he was still sensitive, but not
selfishly so. This can be seen in his concern for
those who followed Jesus. His sensitivity was focused on
God and His glory.

Secondly, it can help to ensure your focus is not always
on yourself. You can get caught up in a vision or a mission
that is bigger than yourself and your particular story –
such as a ministry in which your church is involved. Doing
this will help you gain a bigger perspective – and you will
more easily be able to see God's view of the overall picture.

FURTHER STUDY

Phil. 2:1-4;
James 1:22-27

1. Whose interests should we look to?

2. What does pure religion involve?

**Gracious Father, help me today to surrender my sensitivity to
You. Now that You have it – it's Yours. Use it for Your honour and
glory. In Jesus' name I pray. Amen.**

NEXT ISSUE

Bringing down giants

Each one of us can struggle with 'giants' that stop us growing spiritually. But are we aware of the 'smooth stones' that God has equipped us with to bring them down?

In this issue, Selwyn looks at some of the biggest giants that can hinder our spiritual walk. Tackling such topics as fear, jealousy, desire, shame, pride, revenge and self-pity he reveals their intimidation tactics as well as the ways in which God teaches us to fight them.

Beginning and ending with the example of David bringing down the giant Philistine Goliath, Selwyn also reveals how Jesus and other biblical characters dealt with such 'giants' - and how we can remove them from our lives once and for all.

NOV/DEC 2014

Every Day with Jesus

Bringing down giants

'The weapons we fight with are not the weapons of the world. On the contrary, they have divine power to demolish strongholds.'
2 Corinthians 10:4

Be revived and refreshed by God's Word   **CWR**

Also available as eBook/ eSubscription

OBTAIN YOUR COPY FROM
CWR, a Christian bookshop or National Distributor.
If you would like to take out a subscription, see the order form at the back of these notes.

Face it, deal with it, leave it

FOR READING & MEDITATION - EPHESIANS 4:17-25

'put off your old self, which is being corrupted by its deceitful desires … and … put on the new self' (vv22,24)

For one more day we will think about the issue of self-pity. Psychologists often point out that the word 'emotion' implies a movement outwards. Pity, according to their theory, should go out to others. When it is turned inwards it becomes self-pity. We live in a world that is longing to be loved; it is not seemly or kind or just to expend pity upon ourselves. A self-pitying self is a pitiful self. So determine today to have done with it.

This brings me to my third suggestion for dealing with self-pity: make a positive decision to look out for any thought of self-pity and consciously reject it. Put your confidence in God and ask Him to help you face it. Bring it to Him and deal with it then and there – forever.

FURTHER STUDY

Mark 6:34-44;
2 Cor. 1:3-11

1. Contrast the attitudes of Jesus and His disciples.

2. Why might we experience troubles?

Teresa of Avila, the sixteenth-century Spanish mystic and author, is said to have battled with constant ill-health and complained of 'rushing waterfalls within her head'. Yet nothing daunted her courage. Her biographer writes: 'When she thought how utterly out of proportion were the tasks laid upon her to her bodily strength, she would laugh to herself, so absurd did it seem.'

Fourth, and finally: let Jesus brand His mark of confidence and trust in God into you. As we have seen, Jesus' branding is a matter of mutual agreement and co-operation. Jesus wants to free you from self-concern and self-compassion; the question is – do you want to be freed? If you do, then bow before Him now and bring to His feet all your thinking and resolve during the past week with this personal prayer:

My Father and my God, I see so clearly that a self-pitying self is a pitiful self. From today forward I want to replace self-pity with Your brand of confidence and trust. For Your own dear name's sake. Amen.

Prayerful dependence

FOR READING & MEDITATION - LUKE 6:1-16

'One of those days Jesus went out to a mountainside to pray, and
spent the night praying to God.' (v12)

Continuing our study of some of the different brand
marks of Jesus with which we are to be branded,
the next characteristic of Jesus we come to is this: His
prayerful dependence upon God. I am sure you will agree
that Jesus Christ was the greatest pray-er the world has
ever seen. He rises head and shoulders above all the other
prayer warriors of Scripture – Abraham, Moses, Daniel,
David and even the great apostle Paul.

Some find it difficult to understand why Jesus ever
needed to pray. They say: 'If He was God then surely He
would have known exactly what to do in every
circumstance. What need did He have for personal
prayer?' To answer this we need to explore the
truth of Jesus' 'humiliation' – His willingness
to lay aside the attributes of Deity and instead
obtain His guidance from God through the power
of believing prayer.

The Message translates verse II of this passage
in this way: 'They were beside themselves with
anger, and started plotting how they might get
even with him.' Here was an obstacle – the
madness of His opponents, which drove them to
consider what they would do to Jesus. They felt,
no doubt, that they had the final say. But over
against that, Jesus had recourse to His Father through
prayer. They consulted each other as to what they would
do to Jesus, and Jesus consulted His Father as to what He
would do through Him. Prayer made it possible for Jesus
not to become a victim of His circumstances. He met His
circumstances in the same way you and I should meet
them – by recourse to God in prayer.

FURTHER STUDY

Ezra 8:21-23;
John 5:19-20;
12:49-50

1. Where was Ezra's dependency?

2. Why did Jesus need to depend on the Father?

**O Father, I too long to come to the point where I depend not on
myself, but on You. Give me the quiet courage and confidence
that Jesus had so that I can meet all my circumstances from
above - with Your help. Amen.**

You decide - through prayer

FOR READING & MEDITATION - ACTS 12:1-17

'So Peter was kept in prison, but the church was earnestly praying
to God for him.' (v5)

We saw yesterday that when some men consulted each other as to what they would do with Jesus, He consulted His Father as to what He would do through Him. Prayer made it possible for Jesus not to become a victim of His circumstances. You are to do the same. This mark of dependence on God through prayer can be stamped into you so that you, too, will meet your circumstances from above - through prayer.

What, I wonder, will your circumstances do to you today? Will they browbeat you, intimidate you, threaten you or cause you to become disheartened? If they do then you could be missing out on God's plans for you. Instead of saying: 'What will my circumstances do to me today?' Rather: 'What shall I do today with my circumstances by prayer?' 'But,' you argue, 'my limitations are many ... they conspire to stifle me and prevent me from being effective.'

FURTHER STUDY

2 Sam. 5:17-25;
Neh. 1:2-4;
2:1-5

1. Why did David use different strategies in battle?

2. What different types of prayer were used by Nehemiah?

Tell me: do limitations have the last word? Not at all. If you trust Jesus with your life then you can decide, through prayer and relationship with God, what you are going to do with your limitations. Many a Christian disciple, spurred on by the fact that she or he has access to God through prayer, has been able to turn a restriction into a revelation. Do not ask today: 'What shall my enemies do with me?' Instead ask: 'What shall I do with my enemies through prayer?' You can have strength to overcome them - to forgive them - if you meet them from above. 'I have power to kill you,' said a Roman judge to a Christian martyr, who replied: 'But I have power to be killed.' Which power was the greater?

O Father, thank You for reminding me that I grow, not just by meeting obstacles in Your name, but through prayer that is induced by those obstacles. I am so deeply thankful. Amen.

'Wake us up to Jesus'

FOR READING & MEDITATION - 2 CORINTHIANS 3:12-18

'And we ... are being transformed into his likeness with
ever-increasing glory' (v18)

Wherever we look at Jesus in the Gospels, it is clear that circumstances did not decide His destiny – prayer did. Herbert Spencer, a famous scientist, once said: 'Whatever amount of power an organism expends in any state is correlative or equivalent to the power taken into it from without.' That natural principle can be transferred to the spiritual realm, and put in this way: our spiritual lives are determined by the power we take into them through prayer.

This is a principle Jesus knew and practised – and so can we. The Saviour was never a victim of circumstances; rather, He was the victor over circumstances – and He managed this victory through constant communion with God in prayer. A student in a theological seminary tells of the profound effect made upon him and others when Kagawa, the Japanese Christian leader who served the destitute in the slums, stood at the front of their class and uttered this prayer: 'O God, may we wake up to Jesus.'

FURTHER STUDY

John 17:1-26

1. How did Jesus face death?

2. What did He pray for?

You see, it's not enough to read the various statements in the Gospels about the prayer life of Jesus, nor is it enough to note the number of times that He prayed. We must 'wake up to Jesus' – in other words, recognise that the only way to live is the way He lived. And how did He live? With absolute confidence in the fact that His prayers were not only heard in heaven, but answered. You can view your prayer life the same way. Someone has called prayer 'life's deepest education'. It is, for in prayer you are educated at the place that counts – the centre of life. You are being educated in being.

O God, wake me up to Jesus. Change me into His image and give me His passion for prayer. I know You are burdening me to pray in order to 'make' me. You inspire prayer in order to answer it. I am so grateful. Amen.

Cause and effect

FOR READING & MEDITATION - LUKE 5:12-26

'Jesus often withdrew to lonely places and prayed ... And the power
of the Lord was present for him to heal' (vv16-17)

Let me quote a part of today's reading from *The Message*:
'Soon a large crowd of people had gathered to listen
and be healed of their ailments. As often as possible Jesus
withdrew to out-of-the-way places for prayer' (vv15-16).
Jesus ran away from the crowds – to pray. We run after
the crowds – and don't pray. Hence we don't attract the
crowds, for people can usually spot someone who has
nothing to give.

During a ministers' seminar some time ago a man
commented: 'We preachers are primarily crowd-conscious,

**FURTHER
STUDY**

Acts 6:2-4;
10:1-6, 9-15

1. How did the
apostles follow
Jesus' example?

2. How did
the Gentiles
come to hear
of Jesus?

and secondarily prayer-conscious. Jesus was
primarily prayer-conscious, and secondarily
crowd-conscious. He both received answers to
prayer and drew the crowds. We do neither.' But
what happened when the crowd finally got to
Jesus? The next verse says: 'The healing power
of God was on him' (v17, *The Message*). The two
things are cause and effect: He 'withdrew to out-
of-the-way places for prayer ... The healing power
of God was on him'. Could something similar be
said of you, or would the comment be: 'He/she
kept in public places and was prayerless ... the
weakness of humanity was present'?

A marvellous story concerning the London slums
of years ago tells how a caring schoolteacher tried to
persuade a group of slum children to clean themselves
up. At first they refused to respond to the appeals. Then
another method was tried. A slum child with a clean face
and clothes was introduced to the group. After this, one by
one, they started to wash their faces. I don't know how it is
with you, but whenever I look into the face of Jesus I soon
realise I must wash my face, my heart, my life.

**Lord Jesus, as I look into Your face today and hear Your voice
speaking to my heart, help me to see that You not only raise the
standard to stupendous heights, but You also supply me with
the power to reach it. Thank You. Amen.**

Why should mortals wonder?

FOR READING & MEDITATION - PSALM 69:13-33

'The LORD hears the needy and does not despise his captive people.'
(v33)

We have been saying that one of Jesus' most notable characteristics was His prayerful dependence upon God. He did not use prayer, as some suggest, in order to benefit from the reflex influence which comes from quiet thought and meditation.

Is prayer only a reflex influence? I believe it is far more. In prayer, my spirit comes in contact with the great Creator of the universe, and the opportunity is given me to come to a common understanding with Him. I am able to adjust my will to His will and, through that relationship, find my personality heightened, my love for Him reinforced and my desire for Him most definitely deepened. In my experience, those who think of prayer only as a reflex influence soon give up on prayer. And no wonder, for as one writer put it: 'It is not possible to project one's spirit continuously toward that which is not responsive.'

A letter I once received asked: 'Can I expect God to give me directions in prayer in the same way that He did with Jesus?' The answer is 'Yes'. He can not only put His directions into our hearts, He can put His very life.

Many authors, poets and philosophers down the years have wondered at whether God speaks in prayer. One poet asked whether we should wonder at this; considering we can hear a radio broadcast across land and sea, a song from over countryside and city, why we should wonder if God speaks through prayer.

I do not wonder – do you?

FURTHER STUDY

2 Chron. 7:14;
20:2-4, 14-22

1. What is God's 'if' condition?

2. How did God respond to Jehoshaphat?

O Father, help me to realise that prayer involves not only me speaking to You, but You speaking to me. Speak to me today, in the same clear way that You spoke to Your Son. For His dear name's sake I ask it. Amen.

Building a vital prayer life

FOR READING & MEDITATION - PSALM 149:1-9

'For the LORD takes delight in his people; he crowns the humble with salvation.' (v4)

Now that we have seen how important prayer was to Jesus, and how necessary it is to have that same characteristic branded into us, we ask ourselves: How do we go about the task of bringing our prayer lives in line with His? Over the years I have given so much advice on the building of one's prayer life that I hesitate to do so again in case I repeat myself unnecessarily. However, here are a few suggestions.

First, determine to become, not a self-dependent being, but a God-dependent being. The only way to achieve this, of course, is through prayer. It may well require a good deal of patience on your part to establish a vital prayer life, but if patience when you fail is necessary in order to learn anything worthwhile then you must determine to be as patient with your failures here as you are in other areas of your life. Remember, the primary reason for prayer is building relationship with God – and with any relationship it takes time, energy and effort.

FURTHER STUDY

Luke 11:1-4;
Acts 2:42-47;
Col. 4:2-4

1. What was the desire of the disciples?

2. What did the Early Church devote themselves to?

Second, breathe a prayer for God's help as you endeavour to increase and deepen your prayer life. Whenever you seek to become more dependent upon God through prayer, you are beginning something which will make the difference between weakness and strength, defeat and victory. The devil knows this, and so he will use every means he can to deter you in your quest. Just as a tiger seeks to slit the throat of its victim so that it cannot breathe, so Satan will aim to disable you when you pray. But have no fear: given your consent and co-operation, God will move heaven and earth in order to help you become proficient in prayer.

O God, help me as I seek to become more proficient in life's most important exercise - prayer. If I stumble, then I shall stumble in Your direction, and if I fall, I shall fall upon my knees. Amen.

More steps to prayer

FOR READING & MEDITATION - 2 CHRONICLES 15:1-15

'The LORD is with you when you are with him. If you seek him, he will be found by you' (v2)

We spend one final day considering the steps we take to develop a closer relationship with God in prayer. Thirdly, realise that God hears your prayer and that He will give to you according to your need – not necessarily what you ask, but what you need. God has promised to supply 'all your needs' (Phil. 4:19), not all your requests. He may give you something better than you ask, or different from what you ask. He may even say 'No', but His 'Nos' are just as loving as His 'Yeses'.

Fourth, take charge of your time! Decide how much time you can give to prayer, and organise your day around this time. Don't let your day decide your prayer time; let your prayer time decide your day. Fix the time and keep it fixed so that you do not have to think about the matter each day. Don't be afraid to relax this rule, however, if circumstances dictate, but try to keep to it as far as you can. Those who benefit from a rich prayer life say that if they don't make time to pray, they end up not having any time to pray.

Fifth, begin your prayer time, if you can, by reading from the Bible. This advice was given to me over 50 years ago, and I have found it to be the most valuable piece of advice I have ever received. Let God speak to you from His Word before you speak to Him through your words. It gives what one preacher calls a 'climate' to your prayer time – it starts you thinking in the right direction.

Are you ready now to be branded with this mark of Jesus – prayerful dependence upon God? God-dependence, rather than self-dependence, is to be infused within you.

FURTHER STUDY

Luke 18:1-14; Phil. 4:6-7

1. What did Jesus recognise about people's prayer lives?

2. How should we pray?

Lord Jesus, I bow yet again before You to have this brand infused into my inner being. Self-dependence is to have no place in my life as I bear branded within me the mark of God-dependence. I am so thankful. Amen.

Joy! Joy! Joy!

FOR READING & MEDITATION – JOHN 15:1-17

'I have told you this so that my joy may be in you and that your joy may be complete.' (v11)

Now we come to the last in our list of the marks of Jesus with which we are to be branded – abundant, overflowing joy. Rendell Harris says: 'Joy is the strength of the people of God; it is their glory, it is their characteristic mark. And when the mark is absent then the characteristic of a Christian is absent.' Strong words! Leaders are often at pains to point out that joy should not be mistaken for happiness. 'Happiness depends on what happens,' they declare, 'but joy is independent of circumstances.'

A question I am often asked in correspondence is this: 'Was Jesus a really joyful person? We read in several different places in the Gospels that He cried, but not once do we read that He laughed.' The reply I give to that question is as follows: 'I don't know whether or not Jesus ever laughed, but He has certainly created me so that I can laugh. And I cannot believe that He, who created laughter, did not laugh Himself!'

FURTHER STUDY

Neh. 8:9-10;
Psa. 2:1-6

1. What is our source of strength?

2. Identify some of the characteristics of God.

However, it is not so much laughter we are thinking of, but joy. That Jesus knew what it was to be joyful is made clear by our text for today. Listen to the wording used in the Living Bible: 'I have told you this so that you will be filled with my joy. Yes, your cup of joy will overflow!' This suggests that although Jesus' joy and our joy are different, they are not alien but allied. You cannot take His joy without finding your own joy complete. You and I can be branded also with this mark of Jesus. His overflowing joy is to be so infused within us that although we will experience sadness, we shall never be overcome by them.

O Father, I am so grateful that in You I can find a joy that makes my own joy complete. I bow in speechless adoration at the wonder of it, and shall be eternally grateful. Amen.

The joy of the redeemed

FOR READING & MEDITATION - PSALM 30:1-12

'You turned my wailing into dancing; you removed my sackcloth and clothed me with joy' (v11)

Yesterday we said that joy – abundant, infectious, overflowing joy – is one of the central characteristics of the Christian faith. Jesus lived it – and so can we. Yet many Christians know little or nothing of a deep, lasting joy. They function by duty rather than by delight – they are artificial rather than artesian. Someone said of such Christians: 'They creak in soul and body on the way to glory.'

Sadly, some Christians not only fail to expect joy to be evident in their lives: they don't even want it. Moffatt translates Romans 5:1 in this way: 'Let us enjoy the peace we have with God'. Can it be that some people have peace with God but don't enjoy it? One commentator says of this verse: 'Some people's peace is a peace without a bubble in it – it doesn't boil and overflow.' In another passage Paul writes: 'We enjoy our redemption' (Eph. 1:7, Moffatt). To be redeemed and not enjoy redemption is a contradiction in terms; joy is inevitable in the heart of a truly redeemed Christian.

However did the infectious faith of Jesus become associated with gloom, frowns and mirthlessness? Some Christian historians believe that the people known as 'Puritans' had something to do with it. The Puritans, of course, were good people but it cannot be denied that they fostered a tradition of sobriety. They thought God frowned on joyful exuberance and they made life solemn. One woman who attended a Billy Graham crusade held in Britain in the 1980s remarked when she saw the joyful crowds: 'Strange, I never associated God with joy before.' Now converted herself, she says: 'I have never been so happy.'

FURTHER STUDY

Psa. 16:5-11; Isa. 12:1-6

1. What is experienced in the presence of God?

2. What is our source of joy?

Father, I am so grateful that redemption extends to the roots of my being, and that my happiness is not dependent on happenings, but upon my relationship with You that persists amid all happenings. Amen.

Inexpressible joy!

FOR READING & MEDITATION - 1 PETER 1:1-9

'though you do not see him now, you believe in him and are filled
with an inexpressible and glorious joy' (v8)

Those who are branded with the joy of Christ are not
only truly joyous, but sometimes hilariously joyous.
Dr Farmer, a church organist, told how he once adjudicated
at a great music festival and heard a Salvation Army
band in action. His musical sensibilities were offended by
both the drummer and the French horn player. When he
pleaded with the drummer not to hit the drum so hard, the
beaming bandsman replied: 'Sir, I'm so happy I could burst
the jolly old drum.' Dr Farmer then turned to the French
horn player and made the same appeal. The enthusiastic
horn player said: 'But sir, I'm so full of joy I could
blow this thing until it is straight.'

**FURTHER
STUDY**

2 Sam. 6:14-16;
Phil. 4:4;
1 Thess. 5:16-19

1. Contrast
the attitudes
of David and
Michal.

2. What is God's
will for us?

It is a sad reflection on today's Church that
exuberance and devotion are regarded as things
that cannot flow together. They can. During the
dark days of World War II a London preacher
wrote: 'It is only when the fires in the individual
heart, or in the denomination, are dying down
that convention frowns on exuberance, and an
air of superiority is affected towards those who
cannot restrain their primitive joy.' The joy of
Jesus need not depart from us, even in the face of
extreme suffering. Drink deep of the life of Jesus,
and you will know the experience of which Charles Wesley
wrote:

My God, I am Thine; what a comfort divine,
What a blessing to know that my Jesus is mine!
In the heavenly Lamb, thrice happy I am,
And my heart it doth dance at the sound of His Name.

Dance? If you can't dance then settle for shouting 'Praise
the Lord!'

**O God, You have everything so wonderfully sorted out for me -
including joy. And especially joy! Help me to take it, for it is my
birthright - and not only take it, but live it. Amen.**

Womb, gloom, tomb!

FOR READING & MEDITATION - ISAIAH 35:1-10

'the ransomed of the LORD will return. They will enter Zion with
singing; everlasting joy will crown their heads.' (v10)

A preacher once remarked: 'The biography of many
people can be summed up in three words: womb,
gloom and tomb. Between the womb and the tomb they
live in gloom.' That is not how we were designed to live.

When a minister went to a certain psychiatrist
complaining of deep feelings of melancholy the
psychiatrist challenged him with this question: 'You
have a faith, haven't you?' To this the minister replied:
'Yes, I have.' 'Then why don't you use it?' the psychiatrist
asked. Psychiatrists are not usually as blunt as that, but
this one evidently knew what he was doing, for
his words had the desired effect. The minister
said: 'Thanks for the prescription. I'll do
precisely that.' He then went out into the street
and shouted at the top of his voice 'Hallelujah!'
His melancholy left him – and never returned. I
am not suggesting, of course, that melancholy or
depression can always be dissolved as easily as
that, but in this minister's case, it was. He made
up his mind to draw upon his faith in Jesus, and
in response to his action of walking into
the street and shouting 'Hallelujah!' something
broke within his soul.

**FURTHER
STUDY**

Luke 2:8-14;
Rev. 19:1-9

1. What has
interrupted our
journey from
womb to tomb?

2. Why can
we shout
hallelujah?

A drama student, seeing the radiant face of a Christian
doctor, commented to a friend: 'I'd be a Christian if I could
be as joyful as him.' Not a high motive, perhaps – but it
shows that people want to get away from the dullness of
life. And one of the things that Jesus brings is deliverance
from dullness and dejection. He imparts overflowing,
exuberant, abundant joy. Indeed, He not only imparts it,
but brands it into us.

**Father, brand me so deeply with Your overflowing joy that my life
history shall not be womb, gloom and tomb, but birth, bloom and
blessedness. For Your own dear name's sake. Amen.**

'Dying kicks of evil habits'

FOR READING & MEDITATION – ACTS 11:1-18

'the Spirit told me to go with them, making no distinction' (v12 RSV)

Today is the last day of our meditations on the brand marks of Jesus. Perhaps, over the past two months, as we have talked about being branded with Christ's characteristics in order to show we belong to Him, you have questioned the absoluteness of the deliverance depicted in these studies.

The power of Jesus to deliver – and deliver instantaneously – is a truth which the New Testament everywhere affirms. But although instantaneous deliverance is possible, it does not always happen that way. Sometimes deliverance is gradual. This is due not to any deficiency on God's part. It often takes time to work through the consequences of previous life choices and because of that, some words of encouragement are necessary. Peter, on the Day of Pentecost, had many inadequacies burned out of him as the fire of the Holy Spirit fell, but some things still lingered – racial prejudice, for example. A special aftertouch was needed to root that out. The record says: 'The Spirit told me to have no hesitation about going with them' (Acts 11:12).

FURTHER STUDY

2 Cor. 4:16-18; 6:3-10

1. Why did Paul not lose heart?

2. How could he rejoice in suffering?

Often there is a little mopping up to be done even after the citadel has been captured by Jesus. A preacher once referred to the areas of resistance that remain as 'the dying kicks of evil habits'. But don't be discouraged – the kicks are dying kicks. You have asked God to brand you with the marks of Jesus – now believe that you have received all that you have asked for. And if there are some 'dying kicks', then remember that you belong, not to a defeated yesterday, but to a victorious present.

My God and Father, help me not to have doubts if my deliverance is not as decisive as I might expect. Remind me that when evil kicks back, the kicks are dying kicks. I move forward now in faith – towards full victory. Amen.

ORDER FORM

4 EASY WAYS TO ORDER:

1. Phone in your credit card order: **01252 784700** (Mon-Fri, 9.30am - 5pm)

2. Visit our online store at **www.cwr.org.uk/store**

3. Send this form together with your payment to:
   CWR, Waverley Abbey House, Waverley Lane, Farnham, Surrey GU9 8EP

4. Visit your local Christian bookshop

For a list of our National Distributors, who supply countries outside the UK, visit www.cwr.org.uk/distributors

YOUR DETAILS (REQUIRED FOR ORDERS AND DONATIONS)

Full Name:

CWR ID No. (if known):

Home Address:

Postcode:

Telephone No. (for queries):

Email:

PUBLICATIONS

TITLE	QTY	PRICE	TOTAL
		Total publications	

All CWR adult Bible-reading notes are also available in eBook and email subscription format.
Visit www.cwr.org.uk for further information.

UK p&p: up to £24.99 = **£2.99**; £25.00 and over = **FREE**

Elsewhere p&p: up to £10 = **£4.95**; £10.01 - £50 = **£6.95**; £50.01 - £99.99 = **£10**; £100 and over = **£30**

Please allow 14 days for delivery   **Total publications and p&p A**

SUBSCRIPTIONS* (NON DIRECT DEBIT)	QTY	PRICE (INCLUDING P&P)			TOTAL
		UK	Europe	Elsewhere	
Every Day with Jesus (1yr, 6 issues)		£15.95	£19.95	Please contact nearest National Distributor or CWR direct	
Large Print *Every Day with Jesus* (1yr, 6 issues)		£15.95	£19.95		
Inspiring Women Every Day (1yr, 6 issues)		£15.95	£19.95		
Life Every Day (Jeff Lucas) (1yr, 6 issues)		£15.95	£19.95		
Cover to Cover Every Day (1yr, 6 issues)		£15.95	£19.95		
Mettle: 14-18s (1yr, 3 issues)		£14.50	£16.60		
YP's: 11-15s (1yr, 6 issues)		£15.95	£19.95		
Topz: 7-11s (1yr, 6 issues)		£15.95	£19.95		
Total Subscriptions (Subscription prices already include postage and packing) **B**					

Please circle which bimonthly issue you would like your subscription to commence from:
Jan/Feb Mar/Apr May/Jun Jul/Aug Sep/Oct Nov/Dec

* Only use this section for subscriptions paid for by credit/debit card or
cheque. For Direct Debit subscriptions see overleaf.

CONTINUED OVERLEAF »

« SEE PREVIOUS PAGE FOR START OF ORDER FORM

PAYMENT DETAILS

☐ I enclose a cheque/PO made payable to CWR for the amount of: **£** _____

☐ Please charge my credit/debit card.

Cardholder's Name (in BLOCK CAPITALS) _____

Card No. ☐☐☐☐ ☐☐☐☐ ☐☐☐☐ ☐☐☐☐

Expires End ☐☐ ☐☐   Security Code ☐☐☐

GIFT TO CWR   ☐ Please send me an acknowledgement of my gift   **C** ☐

GIFT AID (YOUR HOME ADDRESS REQUIRED, SEE OVERLEAF)

giftaid it

I am a UK taxpayer and want CWR to reclaim the tax on all my donations for the four years prior to this year **and on** all donations I make from the date of this Gift Aid declaration until further notice.*

Taxpayer's Full Name (in BLOCK CAPITALS) _____

Signature _____ **Date** _____

*I understand I must pay an amount of Income/Capital Gains Tax at least equal to the tax the charity reclaims in the tax year.

GRAND TOTAL (Total of A, B, & C) ☐

SUBSCRIPTIONS BY DIRECT DEBIT (UK BANK ACCOUNT HOLDERS ONLY)

Subscriptions cost £15.95 (except *Mettle*: £14.50) for one year for delivery within the UK. Please tick relevant boxes and fill in the form below

☐ *Every Day with Jesus* (1yr, 6 issues)
☐ Large Print *Every Day with Jesus* (1yr, 6 issues)
☐ *Inspiring Women Every Day* (1yr, 6 issues)
☐ *Life Every Day* (Jeff Lucas) (1yr, 6 issues)

☐ *Cover to Cover Every Day* (1yr, 6 issues)
☐ *Mettle*: 14-18s (1yr, 3 issues)
☐ *YP's*: 11-15s (1yr, 6 issues)
☐ *Topz*: 7-11s (1yr, 6 issues)

Issue to commence from:
☐ Jan/Feb ☐ Jul/Aug
☐ Mar/Apr ☐ Sep/Oct
☐ May/Jun ☐ Nov/Dec

CWR

Instruction to your Bank or Building Society to pay by Direct Debit

DIRECT Debit

Please fill in the form and send to: CWR, Waverley Abbey House, Waverley Lane, Farnham, Surrey GU9 8EP

Name and full postal address of your Bank or Building Society

To: The Manager   Bank/Building Society

Address

_____

_____

_____ Postcode

Name(s) of Account Holder(s)

Branch Sort Code ☐☐ ☐☐ ☐☐

Bank/Building Society Account Number ☐☐☐☐☐☐☐☐

Originator's Identification Number

4	2	0	4	8	7

Reference
☐☐☐☐☐☐☐☐☐☐

Instruction to your Bank or Building Society
Please pay CWR Direct Debits from the account detailed in this Instruction subject to the safeguards assured by the Direct Debit Guarantee.
I understand that this Instruction may remain with CWR and, if so, details will be passed electronically to my Bank/Building Society.

Signature(s)

_____

Date

Banks and Building Societies may not accept Direct Debit Instructions for some types of account